W9-DJM-593

Pakistan and the Bomb

Notre Dame Studies on International Peace
Joan B. Kroc Institute for International Peace Studies
University of Notre Dame

With the end of the cold war the promise and relevance of peace research have significantly increased. The issues now addressed include the nature of the world order, international institutions, the resolution of deadly conflicts, humanitarian security, and ethical issues raised by violence, environmental degradation, and poverty. Peace studies probe these problems and search for comprehensive solutions.

The *Notre Dame Studies on International Peace* series focuses on these vital issues. Scholarly perspectives are combined with sound policy recommendations and the setting of normative standards. The books published here emanate primarily from the research work of the Kroc Institute and its other activities, especially the annual Theodore M. Hesburgh, C.S.C., Lectures on Ethics and Public Policy.

Previously published in the series *Notre Dame Studies on International Peace* are *India and the Bomb: Public Opinion and Nuclear Options,* edited by David Cortright and Amitabh Mattoo; *The Ethics and Politics of Humanitarian Intervention,* by Stanley Hoffmann (the 1995 Hesburgh Lectures); and *New Wine and Old Bottles: International Politics and Ethical Discourse,* by Jean Bethke Elshtain.

The Joan B. Kroc Institute for International Peace Studies was established at the University of Notre Dame in 1986. In addition to research projects, the Institute has an international graduate program and an undergraduate concentration in peace studies. It is a premier institution in its field in the United States. More information can be obtained from the Kroc Institute, P.O. Box 639, University of Notre Dame, Notre Dame, Indiana, 46556-0639, USA (phone 219-631-6970; fax 219-631-6973).

Pakistan and the Bomb
Public Opinion and Nuclear Options

EDITED BY
Samina Ahmed
and David Cortright

WITH A PREFACE BY
Raimo Väyrynen

University of Notre Dame Press
NOTRE DAME, INDIANA

Copyright © 1998
University of Notre Dame Press
Notre Dame, Indiana
All Rights Reserved

Manufactured in the United States of America

Library of Congress Cataloging-in-Publication Data

Pakistan and the bomb: public opinion and nuclear options / edited by
Samina Ahmed and David Cortright; with a preface by Raimo Väyrynen.
    p.   cm. — (Notre Dame studies on international peace)
  ISBN 0-268-03818-X (alk. paper). —ISBN 0-268-03819-8 (pbk.;
alk. paper)
  1. Nuclear weapons—Government policy—Pakistan. 2. Nuclear
weapons—Pakistan—Public Opnion. 3. Public opinion—Pakistan.
I. Ahmed, Samina-1952-   . II. Cortright, David, 1946-
III. Series.
UA853.P3P3   1998
355.02'17'095491—dc21   97-3802
                                                     CIP

♾ The paper used in this publication meets the minimum requirements of the
American National Standard for Information Sciences—Permanence of
Paper for Printed Library Materials, ANSI Z39.48-1984

Contents

Preface

The cold war showed decisively that nuclear weapons programs create their own military, bureaucratic, and economic constituencies in whose self-interest it is to advocate the continuation of these programs. The roots of nuclear arms races are as much domestic as based on security threats and political rivalries between the participating states. Special interest groups created by the acquisition of nuclear weapons dominate not only in the established nuclear weapons powers, but also in the threshold countries involved in their development. In most cases political leaders have only limited control or no control at all over the "nuclear barons."

Such "nuclear estates" also exist in South Asia. In an earlier study, *India and the Bomb: Public Opinion and Nuclear Options* (University of Notre Dame Press, 1996), David Cortright and his collaborators showed how widely spread among the Indian elites are the pronuclear views of its military-scientific estate. Cortright, Samina Ahmed, and other contributors make similar findings, stressing especially the strong position of the Pakistani army, in this sequel on the South Asian nuclear dilemma, *Pakistan and the Bomb*. Like the earlier volume, it is based on unique elite interviews conducted under the auspices of the Joan B. Kroc Institute for International Peace Studies at the University of Notre Dame and the Fourth Freedom Forum.

As in India, the Pakistani elite opinion favors nuclear ambiguity to either overt weaponization or the total renunciation of nuclear weapons. The authors argue that Pakistan should try to avoid an open-ended nuclear arms race with India. The reason is simple: as a smaller country, the costs of such an arms race would be much higher for Pakistan than India. Moreover, as a technologically weaker country, Pakistan has no chance to emerge as a military winner from the potential nuclear rivalry with India. One should also keep in mind, as shown by Ahmed and Cortright, that the weaponization option contains significant technological and security risks.

From this perspective, it would be rational for Pakistan to advocate the complete elimination of nuclear weapons in South Asia. A critical question is whether Pakistan should make a unilateral move, as Zia Mian suggests, to renounce its bomb-making capability. Opponents of such a unilateral move can easily argue that it would leave Pakistan at the mercy of its larger neighbor. On the other hand, such a move would deprive the Indian "nuclear estate" of a main justification for the bomb, i.e., that it is needed for security reasons to counter the Pakistani bomb plans.

A Pakistani renunciation of its nuclear weapons capability would reveal that India sees its bomb more in a global than in a regional context, as a political equalizer with other major powers of the world. Thus, the asymmetries between India and Pakistan derive not only from difference in size and the level of technology, but from differences in political alignment. This helps to explain why Pakistan seeks greater external support, especially from China.

The preference for nuclear ambiguity seems to mean, as Pervez Hoodbhoy argues, that Pakistan is likely to cap its nuclear program. If the Indian preference is the same, an open-ended nuclear arms race in South Asia can be averted and an existential nuclear deterrence substituted for full weaponization. But the relationship of nuclear deterrence, whether explicit or implicit, can never be stable. Therefore, nuclear ambiguity needs, as Zahid Hussain points out, constant political nurturing: conflict resolution, especially in Kashmir, confidence building, and preventive diplomatic action.

A major problem is that these political remedies have to be applied mainly by the politicians of both sides, while the bomb technologies are controlled by the military and bureaucratic "nuclear estates." Especially if India and Pakistan possess or acquire active, clandestine nuclear weapons, the plans for their potential use are controlled by the military and are thus largely unaccountable. To avert the menace of regional nuclear war, therefore, it is necessary to make the "nuclear estate" much more accountable by increasing civilian control. Even this is only a partial solution, however, as the stability and peace orientation of the political leadership can be guaranteed neither in India nor Pakistan.

The focus on South Asia should not, of course, deflect attention from the arsenals of the established nuclear weapons powers, especially Russia and the United States. The problems of cutting back and controlling these weapons continue to be formidable. Both *India and the Bomb* and *Pakistan and the Bomb* show in a detailed and convincing manner that the South Asian elites have committed themselves to nuclear weapons under conditions in which risks and instabilities are real.

These path-breaking elite surveys should provide a mirror to the global and local "nuclear estates" that show ultimately that there is no safety in weapons of mass destruction. While nuclear arsenals will not be dismantled immediately, the studies painstakingly organized by Samina Ahmed and David Cortright show that there are not only risks, but also opportunities.

The presence of choices should encourage reflection and the weighing of alternatives among those who are responsible. In the end, politics and science in South Asia and elsewhere should aim at the eradication of poverty, which remains the biggest global scourge, and not at the accumulation of the means of mass annihilation.

Raimo Väyrynen
Joan B. Kroc Institute for International Peace Studies
University of Notre Dame
November 1997

Foreword

India's nuclear weapons tests of May 1998 and Pakistan's decision to follow suit have fundamentally altered the security landscape of South Asia and the world. Suddenly the nuclear club has jumped from six (the five declared nuclear weapons states plus Israel) to eight and the dangers of horizontal proliferation have increased. In South Asia, an overt nuclear arms race looms. The nuclear postures of India and Pakistan have gone from calculated ambiguity to overt weaponization. It is likely that the decision to test weapons will be followed by a commitment to deploy such weapons on aircraft, missiles and perhaps even at sea. In combination with rising political animosities and the ballistic missile competition already underway, the new nuclear competition threatens to plunge the subcontinent into war and raises the danger of a nuclear holocaust.

The research and writing for this book were completed prior to the latest alarming developments in South Asia. Indeed, the nuclear tests by India and Pakistan came just as the text was entering final production. Rather than rewriting the book, we decided to proceed quickly with production, believing that the book remains highly relevant and indeed has taken on new importance. Only in chapter 5, which examines the consequences of nuclear weaponization, have we made a few changes in the manuscript to account for the relevant events. Otherwise the book remains unchanged.

This volume helps to explain how Pakistan reached its current state of nuclear competition with India. The book also offers perspectives and strategies for reversing the nuclear arms race in South Asia. Chapters 3 and 5 in particular explain the hazards of proceeding on the path of nuclear development and present arguments and policy options for avoiding these dangers. The volume explains Pakistan's journey to nuclear weapons capability from multiple perspectives: the experience of three wars with India, culminating in Pakistan's dismemberment in 1971; the decision to build the bomb and the twenty-five-year history of its development; the dominance of political decision making by the Pakistan armed forces; the distorted and often misinformed state of public opinion; the desire to overcome social and economic backwardness, and the inconsistent and often troubled relationship with the United States. These and other factors provide the background for Pakistan's decision to develop a nuclear weapons capability.

In the survey conducted for this book, a substantial number of Pakistani respondents opposed overt weaponization even if India were to conduct an additional nuclear test, indicating a level of public resistance to an overt nuclear arms race. After the nuclear tests and the abandonment of nuclear ambiguity by India and Pakistan in May 1998, the international community must now focus its attention on preventing the further development and deployment of nuclear weapons in the subcontinent. We hope that the volume will enhance understanding of the current nuclear dilemma in South Asia and that it can also offer direction to those searching for ways to restrain Pakistani and Indian nuclear ambitions.

Samina Ahmed and David Cortright
June 1998

Acknowledgments

This book is the product of a collaborative effort on the part of many colleagues and supporters. Stephen P. Cohen at the Program in Arms Control, Disarmament, and International Security at the University of Illinois was an essential inspiration and intellectual guide for this project and for the earlier study of nuclear policy in India. We gratefully acknowledge the financial support that made this project possible. Our greatest debt is to George Perkovich, director of the Secure Society program at the W. Alton Jones Foundation. As a scholar on South Asian security Perkovich recognized the value of this project and offered important advice and encouragement all along the way. As a foundation executive he provided the essential financial backing for the public opinion survey and the commissioning of chapters for the book. We are especially grateful to Howard Brembeck, founder and chairman of the Fourth Freedom Forum, whose vision and generosity have contributed greatly to this project. Brembeck's plan for a safer and more secure world free from the fear of nuclear weapons is the inspiration for this book and all the activities of the Fourth Freedom Forum.

We acknowledge the support and encouragement of our colleagues at the Joan B. Kroc Institute for International Peace Studies at the University of Notre Dame, especially the Institute's director, Dr. Raimo Väyrynen. This volume is the second in a two-part study of public opinion and nuclear policy options in South Asia cosponsored by the Kroc Institute under Väyrynen's direction. The earlier volume, *India and the Bomb: Public Opinion and Nuclear Options*, was also published by the University of Notre Dame Press. George A. Lopez served as advisor for the South Asia project and provided helpful advice, especially in the early stages of the effort. Senior fellow Robert Johansen also offered encouragement and support. We express special thanks to Sandy Krizmanich and Clare White for their help with administrative matters at the Kroc Institute.

The staff at the Fourth Freedom Forum performed the bulk of the support work necessary to turn the manuscript into a completed book. The dedicated efforts of the staff were indispensable to the successful completion of the project. We owe a special debt of thanks to Keith Swartzendruber, who served as research assistant for the Forum. Swartzendruber spent many long hours editing manuscripts, researching documents, and checking citations. He worked closely with us throughout the final stages of the project to prepare the manuscript for production. Jennifer Glick edited the final manuscript and turned it into camera-ready copy for printing. Ann Pedler and Miriam Redsecker at the Forum provided invaluable administrative support.

Many Pakistani colleagues contributed to this effort including: A.H. Nayyar and Ayaz Naseem at Quaid-i-Azam University in Islamabad; Nasir Zaidi at the Documentation Center, *The News*, Islamabad; Mr. Ahmed Khan, who assisted with correspondence; and Hidayat Hasan, senior research analyst at Hagler Bailly Pakistan, Ltd. In Islamabad. We express special thanks to Majid Sheikh, managing director of Saleem Majid Marketing, based in Lahore, that conducted the public opinion survey upon which this volume is based. We also acknowledge the support of our colleague Amitabh Mattoo, School of International Studies at Jawaharlal Nehru University in New Delhi, who coedited the earlier volume on India and encouraged this project as well.We owe special thanks to our contributing authors, Zaheed Hussain of *Newsline* in Karachi, Zia Mian of the Sustainable Development Policy Institute in Islamabad, and Pervez Hoodbhoy of the Physics Department at Quaid-i-Azam University in Islamabad. Their attention to deadlines and patience with our editing helped assure a smooth book production process. We were fortunate to have such skilled and dedicated partners in this endeavor.

We gratefully acknowledge the support of all those who helped in this project, but we take full responsibility for the book's errors and faults. We hope that this volume adds to the knowledge and understanding that can lead to a more peaceful future for the people of South Asia.

Samina Ahmed and David Cortright
Karachi, Pakistan and Goshen, Indiana

About the Contributors

Samina Ahmed is a specialist on South Asian security and a freelance journalist. She has been a visiting scholar at the Cooperative Monitoring Center at Sandia National Laboratories, Albuquerque, New Mexico and has worked at the Pakistan Institute of International Affairs in Karachi and the Institute of Regional Studies in Islamabad. She is a member of the International Research Committee of the Regional Centre for Strategic Studies in Colombo. Her latest publication is "Public Opinion, Democratic Governance and the Making of Pakistani Nuclear Policy," in *Nuclear Weapons and Arms Control in South Asia After the Test Ban*.

David Cortright is the president of the Fourth Freedom Forum in Goshen, Indiana and research fellow at the Joan B. Kroc Institute for International Peace Studies at the University of Notre Dame. He is the editor of *The Price of Peace: Incentives and International Conflict Prevention*.

Pervez Hoodbhoy is professor of high energy and nuclear physics at the Quaid-i-Azam University in Islamabad. He received his Ph.D. from the Massachusetts Institute of Technology in 1978. As an activist for social reform, he has produced two major series for Pakistan television on education issues and popular science, and is the author of *Islam and Science: Religious Orthodoxy and the Battle for Rationality* which has been translated into four languages. He writes and lectures on arms control issues related to the subcontinent.

Zahid Hussain is one of Pakistan's leading journalists on defense and security issues. He is also the senior editor for *Newsline*, Karachi, and a correspondent for the Associated Press. Hussain has been a former visiting fellow at the Stimson Center in Washington, D.C.

Zia Mian is a research associate at the Center for Energy and Environmental Studies at Princeton University. He was a visiting fellow with the Union of Concerned Scientists in Cambridge, Massachusetts and a research fellow at the Sustainable Development Policy Institute in Islamabad. Mian is also the editor of *Pakistan's Atomic Bomb and the Search for Security* and is currently editing a volume on the pathologies of conflict in Pakistani society.

Raimo Väyrynen is the John M. Regan, Jr. director of the Joan B. Kroc Institute for International Peace Studies at the University of Notre Dame. He has published widely on issues of international security.

PAKISTAN
Location of
Polling Sites

Rawalpindi

Peshawar

Islamabad

Quetta

Lahore

Feisalabad

Larkana

Karachi

Pakistan and the Bomb

1

Pakistani Public Opinion and Nuclear Weapons Policy

by Samina Ahmed and David Cortright

The currency of power in the world today is slowly changing. The influence of military and nuclear power is diminishing, while economic, technological, and even cultural factors are assuming increased significance. The global nonproliferation regime has gradually gained strength and legitimacy through new international, regional, and bilateral agreements and verification mechanisms. The United States and Russia have agreed in the START accords to reduce their nuclear arsenals by 60 percent. Five states—South Africa, Argentina, Brazil, Ukraine, and Belarus—have renounced the nuclear option. North Korea has accepted unprecedented international monitoring of its nuclear program. The Nuclear Nonproliferation Treaty (NPT) was indefinitely extended in May 1995, and the Comprehensive Test Ban Treaty (CTBT) was approved by the UN General Assembly in September 1996 with the support of all five declared nuclear weapons states and 153 nonnuclear states.[1]

In South Asia, by contrast, the nuclear weapons option remains under active consideration and shows little sign of receding. Both India and Pakistan have achieved de facto nuclear weapons capability and are engaged in a military and nuclear competition that shows disturbing parallels to the earlier cold war rivalry between the United States and the Soviet Union. Neither country is willing to accept international safeguards on its nuclear activities or to sign the NPT and CTBT agreements. Within Pakistan, policy imperatives, perceptions, and directions remain committed to the nuclear option. According to its policymakers, Pakistan possesses the capability and the infrastructure to develop a nuclear arsenal, although this capability is cloaked in a veil of ambiguity. The first official disclosure of Pakistan's nuclear weapons capability came in February 1992 when Foreign Secretary Shaharyar Khan disclosed in an interview with *The Washington Post* that Pakistan possesses "all the elements which, if hooked together, would

3

become a [nuclear] device."[2] Pakistani officials have consistently claimed since then that, although it will not give up its nuclear option, Pakistan has no intention of developing nuclear weapons. Former prime minister Benazir Bhutto stated, "We do have the knowledge but . . . there is a difference between knowledge and capability. So we do have knowledge, if confronted with a threat, to use. But we do not, in the absence of any threat, intend to use that knowledge."[3] Most recently, Prime Minister Nawaz Sharif declared in a Defense Day speech on 7 September 1997 that "Pakistan's nuclear capability is an established fact."[4]

In recent years, as Indo-Pakistani relations have deteriorated, the internal Pakistani debate has correspondingly hardened. While Pakistani policymakers continue to favor the current posture of nuclear ambiguity, i.e., neither overtly acquiring nor renouncing nuclear weapons, segments of Pakistan's pronuclear elite have begun to press for overt weaponization, oblivious of the dangers that even the present directions of nuclear policy pose to Pakistan's (and India's) security. According to recent reports from U.S. intelligence agencies and the nuclear industry, Pakistan has steadily advanced its nuclear production capacity in recent years.[5] An unsafeguarded plutonium production reactor and reprocessing facility are nearing completion at Khushab.[6] Pakistan has also expanded its uranium enrichment capacity, refined its ability to test atomic bomb designs through computer simulation, and steadily improved its capacity to produce ballistic missiles.[7] In India as well, a hardening of attitudes toward nuclear weapons policy has occurred, as evidenced by New Delhi's 1996 rejection of the CTBT, which it had championed for more than forty years, and its refusal in 1997 even to negotiate a proposed Fissile Material Cutoff Treaty. The new government led by the hawkish Bharatiya Janata Party (BJP) fulfilled its pledge to "induct" nuclear weapons into India's defense policy when it conducted five nuclear tests in May 1998.

International concern about nuclear weapons development and the possible outbreak of hostilities between India and Pakistan is more than justified. Tensions between these two geographically contiguous countries could result in yet another conventional war, and any armed conflict between the now nuclear-capable adversaries carries the possibility, however remote, of nuclear war. The goals of nuclear nonproliferation and conflict prevention in South Asia are thus extremely important and merit priority international attention. This study attempts to address these goals through an in-depth analysis of the current directions of nuclear policy in Pakistan and an examination of the limitations and possibilities inherent in elite public opinion on nuclear policy.

A recent report from a prestigious task force of the U.S. Council on Foreign Relations acknowledges the nuclear danger in South Asia but advocates a new U.S. policy of easing nonproliferation pressures on India and

Pakistan and "establishing a more stable plateau for their nuclear competition."[8] The report calls for greater U.S. engagement with the region and a more frequent use of incentives rather than sanctions in dealing with the two countries. We agree that incentives are generally preferable to sanctions as tools of influence in international affairs,[9] but many of the initiatives recommended by the council task force, such as supplying weapons and military assistance, are likely to be counterproductive to the long-term prospects for democracy and demilitarization. The council's recommendations for incentives to civil society, especially debt forgiveness and support for social welfare,[10] would be more beneficial in generating alternatives to the present military/nuclear dominance of Pakistani policy. The task force's apparent acquiescence to nuclear proliferation belies its acknowledgment of the "explosive" situation in the region.[11] The security risks inherent in the current nuclear competition in South Asia are too great, and the social and economic costs too enormous, to permit such a complacent view. No one would deny the immense challenges involved in attempting to reverse the military and nuclear rivalry between India and Pakistan, but the goal of eliminating the threat of nuclear war in the region should be the constant aim of scholarship and policy. We hope that this volume contributes in some small way to the realization of that objective.

Pakistan's Nuclear Choices

The chapters of this book view Pakistan's nuclear choices and their potential consequences through the prism of an extensive survey of Pakistani elite public opinion that was released in August 1996 specifically for this study. The survey attempts to assess educated opinion on nuclear policy options and also probes the underlying motivations for present attitudes. The survey examines the factors which could convince respondents to change their views on nuclear weapons policy. This chapter contains a summary of the survey. The complete report, along with questions and tabular data, is reproduced as an appendix. The opinion survey examines four major dimensions of Pakistani elite opinion toward nuclear policy: 1) the convergence of elite opinion and official nuclear policy, 2) the extent of support for other than official views, 3) factors influencing the perceptions of Pakistani elites, and 4) conditions that might change opinions on the nuclear option.

In the four chapters that examine Pakistan's nuclear choices, the authors have been given the task of evaluating the strengths and weaknesses of the four main nuclear policy options which are available to Pakistan:

1. maintaining the official policy of nuclear ambiguity, that is, no overt acquisition or renunciation of nuclear weapons;

2. renouncing the nuclear option by abandoning a nuclear weapons program;
3. capping the nuclear program at current levels without reversing nuclear production;
4. going nuclear, or opting for overt weaponization.

An analysis of all four policy options provides a comprehensive account of the advantages and disadvantages embodied in each option.

In chapter 2, Zahid Hussain, senior editor, *Newsline,* a major Pakistani monthly, examines the history as well as the current directions of Pakistan's nuclear posture of ambiguity in light of domestic, regional, and extraregional factors. Assessing the nature of the internal debate between supporters and opponents of official policy, Hussain reaches the conclusion that neither advocates of overt weaponization nor moderates rejecting official policy are likely to influence the character of the nuclear program. Pakistani decision makers will continue to favor the present posture of nuclear ambiguity in the absence of concessions from Pakistan's main regional adversary, India.

In chapter 3, Zia Mian of the Sustainable Development Policy Institute offers an impassioned analysis of the ethical and political contradictions inherent in the current nuclear policy. Mian makes a strong case for the renunciation of Pakistan's nuclear weapons on strategic, political, economic, and environmental grounds. He favors a unilateral renunciation of nuclear weapons as the simplest and most direct approach and as the policy that can best advance Pakistan's national interests in both the internal and external spheres.

In chapter 4, Pervez Hoodbhoy, Department of Physics, Quaid-i-Azam University, explores the future directions of Pakistani nuclear policy and argues that a capping of the nuclear program is likely because of economic and social constraints, while also being desirable from a policy perspective. Hoodbhoy reviews the current costs of the Pakistani nuclear program and emphasizes the enormous additional economic and social burdens that would result from an accelerated nuclear competition with India. Hoodbhoy concludes his chapter with a skeptical review of the various arms control agreements that have been suggested for South Asia, proposing instead a treaty to ban the production of tritium, an essential ingredient for advanced fusion and boosted fission weapons.

In chapter 5, we analyze the pros and cons of the overt weaponization option. Focusing on the interlinked domestic and external factors that have fueled Pakistan's nuclear quest, we examine the political, economic, security-related, and environmental imperatives that are likely to deter policymakers from adopting the weaponization option. We focus particularly on the technological challenges and security risks associated with an unrestrained nuclear competition. The chapter concludes by identifying the elements of Pakistani public opinion that might constrain a drive toward weaponization, and outlining elements of an international strategy for encouraging greater public involvement in the nuclear debate.

Domestic Dilemmas and Public Opinion on Nuclear Options

This study of public opinion and nuclear policy is an attempt to overcome the lack of informed public debate and transparency in Pakistani nuclear decision making. This lack of openness is reflective of the political structure itself. Nuclear policy remains the domain of the Pakistani military, which has been the dominant domestic actor for most of Pakistan's history. There is little or no input on nuclear policy making from senior political leaders and no involvement from the wider public. While civilian actors in the country's powerful bureaucracy, in particular administrators and scientists attached to its nuclear program, play some role in determining the options available, all decision making, including the acceptance or rejection of basic policy options, is exercised by the military establishment. Formal political power was restored to civilian hands in 1988, following eleven years of direct military rule, but elected governments have been weak and have had little voice in the formulation of nuclear weapons policy. In January 1997 a Council for Defence and National Security was established with "advisory" power over all matters of "national interest,"[12] although the powers of the council were later curtailed by the government of Prime Minister Nawaz Sharif. Through all the changes in civilian government and the shifting of bureaucratic structures, the armed forces have retained their place at the heart of Pakistani decision making. As a result, politicians from the two major Pakistani political parties, the Pakistan People's Party (PPP) and the Pakistan Muslim League (Nawaz) (PML-N), have tended to support the military's priorities in the fields of defense and security, including the nuclear domain, in the hope of attaining or retaining the support of the armed forces, a vital factor in the survival of any civilian government. With the internal debate thus confined to declarations of support for the nuclear option, reasoned political debate on the directions of Pakistan's nuclear program is practically nonexistent.

In the absence of informed opinion among elected representatives, public opinion in Pakistan has generally accepted official rhetoric. This internalization of established policy is assisted by prolonged exposure to governmental propaganda conducted via the officially controlled electronic media or through the aegis of sympathetic academics, media personalities, or retired civil and military bureaucrats.[13] Most of the Pakistani population does not play a role in influencing policy making on defense and security issues. Literacy rates are low and political and socioeconomic mobility is restricted by the closed nature of the political system as well as by endemic poverty and underdevelopment.

Pakistan's small middle class does play a role, albeit limited, as the country's opinion-making elite, particularly through an influential and independent print media. This educated elite has, in the past, succeeded in changing internal norms and influencing the directions of domestic politics. The absence of any domestic legitimacy for authoritarian rule, despite the military's dominant position, is one indicator of the influence of this segment of the population. In the nuclear context, Pakistan's educated elite is of particular importance. Any attempt to either open the existing debate on the nuclear option or influence a change in current opinions will inevitably depend on the involvement of this educated elite. The Kroc Institute survey thus specifically targeted educated professionals as a key segment of Pakistani society with the potential for democratizing the debate on nuclear options and perhaps exerting positive influence on the future direction of policy.

Pakistan's Nuclear Policy

In numerous official declarations, aimed both at domestic and international audiences, Pakistani decision makers have asserted that the country's nuclear program is peaceful in nature. They have also claimed that the nuclear program provides a measure of military security against India. Thus ambiguity forms the foundation of Pakistan's past and present nuclear policy, as decision makers reiterate the policy of keeping the nuclear option open—neither renouncing nuclear weapons nor acquiring them. Officials stress that Pakistan's nuclear weapons capability will not be used to create a weapons arsenal, yet they press ahead with a steady enhancement of nuclear capability.

Pakistan's official nuclear policy, as in the Indian case, attempts to simultaneously draw from the vocabulary of nuclear deterrence and nuclear disarmament. On the one hand, officials claim that Pakistan is committed to the ideals of global nuclear disarmament, and that it would favor, as a first step, the denuclearization of its immediate regional environment. On the other hand, Pakistani policymakers and their domestic sympathizers claim that nuclear deterrence, based on ambiguity, is an essential component of Pakistani security. President Zia ul-Haq claimed that the South Asian region has "achieved a stable nuclear deterrent relationship based on ambiguity as to whether India or Pakistan had nuclear weapons, and if they did, how many they possessed."[14]

The context and substance of Pakistan's nuclear policy must be analyzed in the light of internal, regional, and international imperatives. In the internal context, factors ranging from regime legitimacy to center-periphery relations impact on nuclear policy. In the regional context, the directions of Pakistan's nuclear policy are overwhelmingly influenced by the state of its relations with neighboring India, and evolve within the context of developments in India's nuclear program. The international environment has its own impact on Pakistan's nuclear policy, resulting in the acceptance or rejection of particular nuclear options. These internal, regional, and international factors are closely interlinked and cannot be examined in isolation.[15]

As its official managers claim, Pakistan's nuclear policy is indeed reactive in nature, dependent on the directions of its relations with India. Pakistan's nuclear program gradually evolved during the decade of the 1960s under the military regime of General Ayub Khan. In its initial stages, Pakistani nuclear policy focused on establishing a modest infrastructure for a nuclear energy program and acquired a small research reactor and nuclear power plant, both under international safeguards. It was, however, inevitable that the program would acquire a military hue since Pakistan's relations with India, rife with hostility since the end of British colonial rule, continued to deteriorate. Memories of the first abortive adventure in Kashmir in 1948 had not yet abated when the Ayub regime launched another misadventure, based on flawed reasoning, resulting in the Indo-Pakistan war of 1965.

Until the 1965 debacle, the Pakistan military had been disinclined to go the nuclear route. Siding with the West during the peak of the cold war, military officials had become the beneficiaries of large-scale Western military and economic assistance, resulting in a constant expansion of the military establishment and the consolidation of its political standing vis-à-vis potential rivals in the state. Public displeasure over the military's performance in the 1965 war, however, led to growing political opposition to military rule, posing the first tangible threat to the military's long-established dominance. At the same time, hostility toward India reached new heights following the war.

As India's nuclear capabilities and infrastructure expanded, it became increasingly clear to Pakistani policymakers that their chief adversary was well on its way to acquiring the status of a nuclear threshold power. These combined internal and regional imperatives led to a rethinking of the nuclear option. The first references to Pakistan's need for a nuclear military capability were made by Ayub's foreign minister, Zulfiqar Ali Bhutto, who left the government in 1966 but returned later as president and prime minister.[16] Bhutto's pronuclear posture was motivated by hostility toward India, belief in the deterrent value of nuclear weapons, and a desire to attain domestic support through anti-Indian and nationalistic rhetoric.

By the mid-1960s, official interest in the military use of nuclear power began to emerge. Pakistan's refusal to join the NPT in 1968 was a clear indication of its desire to keep its nuclear option open. Pakistan's defeat in the 1971 war and its subsequent dismemberment gave further impetus to the evolution of nuclear policy. In the domestic domain, the decision on the part of the Bengalis to secede created a new crisis of state legitimacy, while India's assistance to Bangladeshi independence and the Pakistani military's humiliating defeat demanded a nationalist response. The Indian nuclear explosion of 1974, which was to confirm Pakistan's doubts about the peaceful nature of Indian nuclear intentions, reinforced the emerging commitment to nuclear weapons development.

In the domestic context the position of the government of Zulfiqar Bhutto was precarious, as the fragile civilian government faced a twofold threat. On the one hand, the PPP government faced multiple challenges to its authority from newly assertive ethnic/regional forces; on the other hand, the civilian leadership was aware of constant threats from a military establishment which had handed over power to civilian hands reluctantly. Bhutto's response was to use the Indian threat to gain domestic support, employing anti-Indian rhetoric for the traditional purpose of diverting and defusing domestic dissent. Bhutto also sought to appease the armed forces, not just by increasing their conventional power but also by attempting to provide them with the nuclear capability possessed by their Indian adversaries. Taking a leaf out of the Indian book, Pakistan worked toward acquiring nuclear weapons capacity, while at the same time launching a diplomatic campaign in support of nonproliferation. Unlike India, however, the Pakistani campaign called for the institution of a regional, as opposed to a global, nonproliferation regime.[17]

There were many problems in the nuclear path that the Bhutto government chose to take. Since the Pakistani nuclear program lagged far behind India in terms of technology and resources, unsuccessful attempts were hastily made to implement an overambitious program through foreign purchases. The international climate proved unsympathetic, however. Although the government was successful in clandestine efforts to acquire centrifuge technology and hardware, its attempt to purchase a French reprocessing plant was blocked.[18] The U.S. Congress passed the Nuclear Nonproliferation Act in 1978, strengthening international mechanisms to prevent the transfer of nuclear explosive technology to nonnuclear states, thereby hampering the Pakistani program. In the mid 1980s Congress passed the Pressler amendment, which became the focal point of U.S.-Pakistani differences over nuclear proliferation for more than a decade. Under the terms of the amendment, U.S. military and economic assistance to Islamabad was to be cut off unless the president certified that Pakistan was not developing and did not possess nuclear weapons.

Under the military regime of General Zia ul-Haq, which deposed and finally executed Bhutto in the late 1970s, Pakistan's nuclear weapons policy proved more successful.[19] As in the past, the directions of Pakistan's nuclear program were dictated by domestic, regional, and international imperatives. Lacking domestic legitimacy and facing widespread political opposition, the regime attempted to gain internal support by adopting a more aggressive and interventionist anti-Indian policy, a policy which was also in line with the military's perceptions and outlook. It then used the Indian threat to justify the directions of Pakistan's nuclear program to both internal and external audiences.[20]

During the Zia regime, nuclear development focused primarily on the enriched uranium route to nuclear weapons and a more aggressive campaign of clandestinely acquiring the necessary technology and hardware. Deteriorating relations with the U.S. during the late 1970s caused considerable concern, since Washington had been a major source of armament and economic assistance, but these misgivings were quickly allayed when the United States reacted to the Soviet invasion of Afghanistan by pouring massive amounts of aid into Pakistan.[21] Washington depended on Islamabad as an essential ally in mobilizing resistance to the Soviets. Choosing to ignore Pakistan's emerging nuclear weapons program, the Reagan administration regularly certified Islamabad's nonnuclear status under the Pressler amendment. The Afghan conflict and the heightening of the second cold war proved to be a bonanza for the armed forces and helped the Pakistani military build up both its conventional and nuclear infrastructures. The acquisition of U.S. F-16s, for example, not only strengthened the firepower of the Pakistani air force, but also provided its military planners with yet another potential nuclear delivery system.[22]

Following Zia's assassination and the end of the cold war, Pakistan's policymakers faced a changed international environment. Former allies such as the United States were no longer willing to ignore the rapid pace of Pakistani nuclearization. In 1990 the Bush administration ended the previous policy of certifying Pakistan's nonnuclear status and imposed Pressler amendment sanctions, thereby embargoing concessional military sales and economic assistance. In a bid to convince the U.S. of Pakistan's benign nuclear intentions, a decision was made to cap Pakistan's uranium enrichment program in 1989. Acknowledging the cap, interim prime minister Moeen Qureshi stated that Pakistan was "not proceeding any further beyond the given point that we have reached in our nuclear program," adding that Pakistan, in any case, was "not working on making any nuclear weapons of any kind."[23] The Bush administration was unconvinced.

Although the U.S. embargo remained in place, these external disincentives proved insufficient to force Pakistani policymakers to reverse or abandon the nuclear option. Pakistan's nuclear managers believed, probably correctly, that even a reversal of the nuclear program would not result in a resumption of the kind of massive American economic assistance received during the cold war. The Pakistani military consistently sought the resumption of the supply of American conventional arms, although with a clear expectation that future sales would no longer be on concessional terms. At the same time the armed forces continued their policy of steadily enhancing the capacity to build nuclear weapons.

From Constraint to Consent

The failure of external pressure to change the directions of Pakistan's nuclear policy is partly related to the lack of a coherent policy among the nuclear weapons states and other major powers on more effective and comprehensive military and economic sanctions. Multilateral agencies, with U.S. approval, provided aid-dependent Pakistan with substantial loans. China and other countries serve as sources of sophisticated conventional arms and nuclear production capability.

U.S. nonproliferation policy has been inconsistent and sent mixed messages to Pakistan's decision makers. The return to a firm policy signaled by the Bush administration in 1990 steadily eroded during the Clinton administration, as Washington once again turned a blind eye to Pakistan's nuclear program. In 1995 the White House won congressional approval for a waiver of the Pressler amendment, allowing the delivery of a $368 million package of weapons and military equipment to Pakistan. Authorization for the arms transfer was provided by the Brown amendment to the 1996 Foreign Assistance Act. Signed into law in early 1996, the Brown amendment not only permitted the delivery of the arms package but allowed future economic and military assistance for "counterterrorism" and other specified purposes. The Brown amendment was intended to encourage nuclear restraint and support Pakistan's role as a moderate Islamic state. Passage of the amendment had no impact on Pakistan's nuclear policy, however. As Prime Minister Benazir Bhutto declared when the arms package was first proposed in 1994, Pakistan will "not accept any unilateral pressure . . . on our peaceful nuclear program."[24] Various domestic actors used the easing of U.S. pressures as a tool to gain internal legitimacy, claiming to have successfully defended the national interest in gaining military assistance without compromising the nuclear program, thereby obtaining an implicit U.S. acceptance of Pakistan's nuclear status.

A further effort to provide military assistance to Pakistan emerged in 1997. In July 1997, the U.S. Senate approved the Harkin-Warner amendment to the Foreign Operation Appropriations Act restoring military training assistance for the Pakistani armed forces under the International

Military and Education Training (IMET) program and providing support for U.S. companies operating in Pakistan under the Overseas Private Investment Corporation (OPIC).[25] The sponsors of the amendment claimed it would strengthen U.S. influence with the Pakistani armed forces, and that this military cooperation would enhance professionalism and civilian control. The result of such programs in Pakistan in the past, however, has been the further strengthening of the legitimacy and influence of the armed forces in a setting where they already have inordinate power. The author of the amendment, Senator Tom Harkin of Iowa, spoke eloquently during the Senate debate of his concern for the "brave people of Pakistan" who suffered under military repression and have struggled for democracy and human rights.[26] Yet the approval of further assistance for the Pakistani armed forces would enhance the power of those who have attacked those "brave people" and who have undermined democracy and human rights. It would also send a message of U.S. consent for the continued development of Pakistan's nuclear program. In November 1997, the House-Senate conference committee on the Foreign Operations Appropriations Act altered the Harkin-Warner amendment. The OPIC provisions were approved, but funding for renewed military training and education was deleted. This action came at the behest of House of Representatives members, especially Nancy Pelosi (D-CA) and David Obey (D-WI), who used the vote to send a message of disapproval at Chinese-Pakistani military and nuclear cooperation.

Domestic Nuclear Politics

In the internal sphere, de facto military dominance of nominally civilian government continues. The military has engineered the removal of civilian governments at will, the latest being the dismissal of the PPP government in November 1996. No elected government has, in fact, been allowed to complete its term of office. The military has, moreover, retained control over all sensitive areas of policy making, while elected leaders and governments, conscious of their vulnerability to military intervention, compete with each other by supporting the military's standpoint on issues ranging from Kashmir to the nuclear program. Politicians and co-opted academics and journalists consistently present the nuclear option as an effective deterrent and a symbol of national sovereignty, thus internalizing official doctrine.[27] This one-sided internal debate increasingly manifests what has been defined as "'nuclearism'—the perception of one's nuclear capability as a general reserve, as a cover against policy blunders and unforeseen contingencies, as an all-purpose security blanket."[28]

The political use of the nuclear option to gain domestic legitimacy or to impugn political opponents has both internal and external implications

for Pakistan's nuclear policy. In the internal context, it is extremely difficult for any major political party to even consider challenging the presumed nuclear consensus, since it would render itself vulnerable to attacks
from its political opponents. In the external sphere, since politicians have
become hostage to their own propaganda, the maneuverability of elected
governments is restricted by the parameters set by the military and domestic sentiment.

The current directions of Pakistan's nuclear program show that international curbs on Pakistani nuclear proliferation have had little effect. The
nuclear program continues unchecked, although Pakistan's official posture remains one of ambiguity. The gradual and incremental changes that
have taken place in Pakistan's position have mostly been in the direction
of a more overt nuclear posture. Pakistani governments have, for instance,
abandoned their previous claims that the program is solely peaceful in
purpose. It is now claimed that Pakistan has succeeded in obtaining its
limited goal of nuclear deterrence vis-à-vis India.

Pakistan's interest in global and regional disarmament is still reiterated at international fora, such as the UN General Assembly and the Conference for Disarmament in Geneva, but Islamabad has remained apart
from recent agreements. Pakistan's refusal to join the nonproliferation regime is still mainly justified on the grounds that India's absence would
threaten Pakistani security. Thus, former prime minister Benazir Bhutto
claimed that Pakistan would sign the NPT "if India does it, simultaneously," while her permanent representative at the UN in Geneva, Munir
Akram, professed that Pakistan favored "the extension of the Treaty because we acknowledge that a breakdown in the NPT consensus would
have negative implications for international stability."[29] During the discussions on the CTBT at the Conference on Disarmament, Pakistan took
the stand that it would not oppose the treaty since it was in favor of nuclear
disarmament, but that it would not sign the treaty unilaterally since, in
the words of Foreign Minister Sardar Aseff Ali, "the CTBT without India
would be meaningless for South Asia."[30] Aware that Indian accession was
unlikely, the conditional Pakistani support for the CTBT was aimed at
gaining international credibility at Indian expense. Even as the delibera-
tions were still taking place, the Muslim League opposition warned the
PPP government that "the people of Pakistan will reject any change of
line on the CTBT since it will amount to giving a strategic walkover to
India on the nuclear issue . . . and permanently place Pakistan at a military, political and strategic disadvantage . . . . "[31] At the same time, Muslim League leader Nawaz Sharif, in a departure from his party's earlier
policy, declared that Pakistan should delink its nuclear program from
India's. Sharif specifically recommended that Pakistan should not sign
the CTBT even if India did so, until its "security concerns are resolved,

Kashmir dispute is settled and no-war pact with India is signed . . . ." This posture was supported by a twenty-five-party conference in August 1996 that comprised almost all major opposition parties.[32]

Following the adoption of the CTBT at the General Assembly's special session in September 1996, the government reiterated its position of support for nuclear disarmament and Indian linkage. President Leghari stated that, "We agree with the treaty in principle and we shall sign . . . the moment India signs because we have great security concern over nuclear activities in our region."[33] A government official claimed that Pakistan's policy of supporting and yet not signing the treaty had provided diplomatic dividends,[34] but in fact the government's statement resulted in accusations of a sellout by the opposition. The Jamaat-i-Islami, an extremist Islamic party, for example, accused the government of "treachery with the nation."[35]

Since the passage of the CTBT, the position of both nuclear advocates and supporters of the nuclear option, as expressed at seminars and through the print media, has veered even more to a delinking of Pakistan's nuclear option from Indian policies. Some now argue that Pakistan's national interests require a retention of its nuclear weapons capability even after an Indian accession to the NPT or the CTBT. The arguments presented to buttress this stance range from the dangers posed to Pakistani security by the conventional arms imbalance vis-à-vis India to the supposed stabilizing effects of nuclear deterrence in South Asia.[36] Some Pakistani nuclear hawks, including former army chief General Khalid Mahmud Arif, have even called for the adoption of a policy of overt weaponization.

There is, as yet, no sign that Pakistan's authoritative decision makers are inclined to adopt an unambiguous, open nuclear posture, since the costs, political, economic, and military, would be too high, as we outline in chapter 5. The increasing assertiveness of pronuclear advocates, however, serves the immediate purposes of Pakistani policymakers, since such domestic sentiment isolates and neutralizes domestic supporters of regional rapprochement and opponents of the nuclear option. The absence of an open debate has contributed significantly to the internalized acceptance of official policies, while the fear of potential repercussions has positively discouraged any pubic questioning of nuclear policy.[37] The effect of Pakistani nuclearism, therefore, is to close off debate on alternatives to current policy and entrench further the already deeply rooted influence of military thinking and military institutions on the determination of both foreign and domestic policy.

The Survey's Findings

The Kroc Institute survey findings provide ample evidence of the extent to which official government policy has been internalized by Pakistani elites. The domestic, regional, and international factors mentioned above have played a significant role in determining elite preferences along lines that largely favor the dominant nuclearist paradigm.

As noted earlier, the Kroc Institute survey specifically targeted educated elites. The respondents were randomly selected from a variety of professions, including academics, lawyers, physicians, journalists, bureaucrats, military personnel, public and private sector executives, sports figures, and artists. The survey was conducted by the Lahore-based firm Saleem Majid Marketing from February 1996 to May 1996. The study method consisted of face-to-face interviews, approximately 20 to 30 minutes long. The sample size was 910 respondents.

Eight cities were selected for the survey, taking into account a number of considerations. The inclusion of Pakistan's main centers of policy making, the federal capital Islamabad and the military general headquarters of Rawalpindi, was essential. The provincial capitals of all four provinces were also selected: Quetta (Baluchistan), Peshawar (Northwest Frontier Province), Lahore (Punjab), and Karachi (Sindh). Feisalabad was selected not only because it is Pakistan's third-largest industrial city, following Karachi and Lahore, but also because its population reflects both a mix of urban and rural Punjab. Since Sindh is ethnically and geographically divided between the Muhajir-dominated urban centers, such as Karachi, and the Sindhi-dominated countryside, an important Sindhi center, Larkana, was also included.

The survey assessed whether Pakistan's policy is consonant with public opinion. It also examined the reasons which motivate particular opinions, as well as those factors that might convince respondents to change their views. The respondents were divided into three categories: (a) supporters of the official governmental policy of keeping the nuclear option open, that is, neither renouncing nuclear weapons nor acquiring them; (b) nuclear advocates, supporting Pakistan's acquisition of nuclear weapons; and (c) nuclear opponents, favoring the renunciation of nuclear weapons. Supporters of government policy were questioned about the factors that would lead them to either support a renunciation of nuclear weapons or opt for an open Pakistani policy of weaponization. Nuclear advocates were asked the reasons behind their support for overt weaponization and the circumstances that might change their opinion on nuclear weapons policy. Nuclear opponents were questioned about the rationale behind their stance and the factors that might lead them to support the acquisition of nuclear weapons. All three categories of respondents were asked to identify conditions that would justify the use of nuclear weapons. The three groups were also questioned about their level of support for an international agreement eliminating nuclear weapons and their assessment of the time frame within which such a treaty could be signed.

The largest group of respondents (61 percent, N=554) supported Pakistan's official policy of keeping the nuclear option open. The second largest group (32 percent, N=290) favored the acquisition of an overt nuclear weapons capability. Both groups based their tacit or overt support of the nuclear option on the perceived threat from India. Only 6 percent of respondents (N=54) favored the renunciation of nuclear weapons. This very limited support for nuclear renunciation does not reflect the full extent of public skepticism about the nuclear option. For example, of those supporting official policy (the largest group), 16 per cent agreed that "under no circumstances" could Pakistan be justified in developing nuclear weapons. It is also important to note that 52 per cent of all respondents disapproved a Pakistani nuclear test, and that 27 percent would oppose such a test even after a second Indian nuclear test. These findings suggest that while nuclear renunciation per se is not a popular option, a considerable minority of Pakistani elites is opposed to nuclearization.

When supporters of government policy were asked what could justify Pakistan developing nuclear weapons, nearly all cited the threat from India, pointing to such factors as an Indian nuclear test and the deployment of Indian ballistic missiles. While supporters of official policy believe that Pakistan should develop nuclear weapons in response to future developments in India, advocates of overt weaponization cite threats from India as the primary reason for developing nuclear weapons. Even nuclear opponents believe that Pakistan would be justified in adopting a policy of weaponization if India were to conduct another nuclear test.

It is not surprising that the dominant factor shaping Pakistani elite opinion on nuclear weapons is the perceived threat from India. Not only have the two countries fought three wars, but the Indian threat has remained the focus of official defense and security policy since Pakistan's inception. Military dominance of the security discourse has emphasized military capability, both conventional and nuclear, as a necessary means to counter that perceived threat. Public opinion has been shaped by this official rhetoric over the past fifty years, resulting in widespread acceptance of the military's threat perception and their proposed means of countering it.

While hostility toward India, suspicion of Indian intentions, and perceptions of the Indian threat were expected findings in the survey, there was a surprisingly high level of support for global disarmament and a remarkable degree of optimism that the international community would successfully negotiate a zero-nuclear regime. As noted earlier, Pakistan's official rhetoric espouses global/regional nondiscriminatory disarmament, but for the most part such rhetoric is aimed at international audiences. The survey indicates that such rhetoric has been accepted at face value by a majority of the Pakistani educated elite. Moreover, the belief that such a treaty could be signed in the near future suggests that many believe in the eventual settlement of Indo-Pakistani differences and the creation of a disarmament and nonproliferation regime at the regional and global levels.

An equally significant finding is the considerable concern voiced by all three groups, including nuclear advocates, about the high environmental cost attached to nuclear production even for peaceful purposes. While the Pakistani government speaks regularly of its concern for disarmament, official rhetoric rarely even mentions the environmental concerns associated with nuclear power. Even within the context of domestic debates, nuclear safety and environmental concerns are largely taboo, or at the most are dismissed because of internal support for nuclear energy or nuclear military capability. The environmental concerns cited in the survey could be attributed, therefore, to the debate on the issue conducted in international fora, both governmental and nongovernmental. The impact of the global media seems to be a factor in the formulation of domestic public opinion. It is likely that the influence of such external factors will grow as international norms on nonproliferation are strengthened and reflected in international discourse. The extent to which the desirability of disarmament or concern about the potential hazards and costs of nuclear power permeate Pakistani elite opinion will depend on the nature of that international discourse, and on the Pakistani government's ability or desire to counter such views.

Detailed Findings

Biographic Characteristics. The respondents, who were randomly selected, were predominantly male (93 percent) reflecting gender inequalities within Pakistan's educated elite. Professional backgrounds did have an impact, albeit limited, on the respondents' views. Although supporters of official policy and, to a lesser degree, advocates of weaponization belonged to all professional categories, no government functionary, including members of the civil and military bureaucracies or the police, favored nuclear disarmament. Most interesting, the highest percentage of nuclear advocates belonged to the business community (54 percent) and to the medical profession (40 percent).

Political Affiliation. Most of the respondents (62 percent) either had no political affiliation or appeared reluctant to disclose it. Of the major political parties, the largest number of respondents citing formal political affiliation (23 percent) belonged to the center-right Pakistan Muslim League (Nawaz), or PML (N), which won an overwhelming parliamentary majority in the February 1997 elections. The Muslim League strongly favors the retention of Pakistan's nuclear weapons program, although 13 percent of those who identified themselves as PML (N) supported nuclear renunciation. Opinions more closely reflected party positions among respondents belonging to leftist parties with a strong regional base. Thus, while there was support among the Pakistan People's Party (PPP) and PML-N respondents for all three nuclear options, there were no nuclear advocates among respondents belonging to the center-left Baluchistan National Party (Bizenjo).[38]

Salience. The nuclear weapons issue had relatively low salience, ranking sixth among issues of potential concern. Regardless of their positions on the nuclear issue, respondents identified the main areas of concern as overwhelmingly domestic in origin, although there was a perceived interrelationship between potential threats to Pakistan's internal and external security. Thus the most urgent issues for the Pakistani elite were Kashmir (56 percent), ethnic conflict and religious sectarianism (54 percent), economic instability (53 percent), poverty (48 percent), and the Afghan refugee presence (43 percent). While the nuclear weapons issue rated below these concerns, 80 percent of all respondents believed the nuclear issue to be "very important." Among the three categories of respondents, all nuclear opponents (100 percent) rated the nuclear issue very important, far higher than their counterparts advocating weaponization (72 percent). This probably reflects nuclear opponents' concerns about the potential dangers posed by Pakistan's nuclear policy.

Availability of Information. Only 1 percent of respondents believed that information on nuclear issues is easily available. Fifty percent of all respondents agreed that information on nuclear issues is "difficult" to get and another 20 percent said such information is "almost impossible to get." Most interesting, 67 percent of supporters of official policy and 82 percent of nuclear advocates believed that it is difficult or impossible to obtain such information, as opposed to 26 percent of nuclear opponents. This could indicate that the information referred to by nuclear opponents is of other than domestic origin, such as information and analyses of the Pakistani nuclear program provided at international fora, on the internet, or in international publications. Exposure to international information sources thus may be associated with opposition to the nuclear option.

Opinion on the Civilian Nuclear Energy Program. A vast majority of respondents (94 percent), regardless of views on nuclear policy, expressed the opinion that a civilian nuclear energy program would help meet Pakistan's energy deficit. Nonetheless, 70 percent of all respondents, again irrespective of their attitudes toward nuclear weapons policy, also believed that the costs of a civilian nuclear energy program far outweigh its benefits. Almost all respondents (92 percent) expressed concern that such programs have high environmental costs attached.

Circumstances Justifying Development of Nuclear Weapons. The survey examined the factors that, in the perceptions of the respondents, would justify Pakistan's development of nuclear weapons. For supporters of official policy, the most important factors were a further development of India's nuclear weapons program. Eighty-five percent cited another Indian test and 72 percent cited the deployment of Indian missiles as sufficient justification for Pakistani weaponization. Some supporters of official policy (36 percent) also cited a future enhancement of Indian conventional arms advantage as a potential justification for weaponization.

All nuclear advocates (100 percent) cited threats from India as the primary justification for Pakistani development of nuclear weapons. Even 54 percent of nuclear opponents felt that Pakistan would be justified in opting for weaponization in the event of another Indian nuclear test. Sixteen percent of official policy supporters and 28 percent of nuclear opponents, however, felt that no circumstance could justify Pakistan's development of nuclear weapons.

No one believed that Pakistan faces a nuclear threat from any other power. Factors such as international prestige and bargaining or threats to the security of the Islamic world were not believed to be acceptable justifications for weaponization. The concept of the Islamic bomb sometimes discussed in the West had no meaning for the survey respondents. Nor was there any significant conviction that weaponization would be justified if Pakistan were to become the target of international economic, political, or military pressure.

Circumstances Under Which Nuclear Weapons Could be Renounced. Among supporters of official policy, changes in Pakistan's relations with India and a reduction of the perceived Indian threat would create conditions under which nuclear weapons could be renounced. An overwhelming majority (71 percent) believed that nuclear weapons could be renounced if the two countries successfully concluded a settlement to resolve the Kashmir dispute. For 49 percent of official supporters, a precondition for renouncing nuclear weapons would be a reduction of India's conventional arms advantage. Forty-two percent would agree to forego the nuclear option following a verifiable renunciation of India's nuclear option. Other factors, such as preferential trade agreements and access to economic aid and advanced technology or the extension of an American and/or Chinese nuclear umbrella, had little or no support as grounds for giving up the nuclear option. However, a considerable number (25 percent) would favor a renunciation of nuclear weapons in the event of a global ban on nuclear tests, a freeze on fissile material production, and a time-bound framework for global disarmament.

Nuclear advocates placed more emphasis than supporters of official policy on a verifiable renunciation of India's nuclear option (87 percent), a final settlement of the Kashmir dispute (81 percent), and a reduction of India's conventional arms advantage (69 percent) as essential preconditions if Pakistan were to renounce nuclear weapons. As opposed to supporters of official policy, nuclear advocates placed less emphasis (18 percent) on steps toward global disarmament. But both groups were in complete agreement that economic and security incentives, such as economic aid or guarantees of nuclear protection from major powers, would not justify a Pakistani renunciation of nuclear weapons in the absence of a settlement of long-standing disputes with India and a reduction of the perceived Indian threat.

Among nuclear opponents, environmental, economic, and moral concerns predominated as justifications against weaponization, while potential threats to Pakistani security were considered to be overstated. An overwhelming majority of nuclear opponents (80 percent) believed that Pakistan should renounce nuclear weapons because nuclear weapons production harms the environment. Another 39 percent felt that nuclear weapons should be renounced because they are morally repugnant, while 17 percent based their opposition to nuclear weapons on the high economic costs involved. The predominance of environmental concerns among nuclear opponents was striking, suggesting that such concerns could provide a basis for building a broader public opposition to the nuclear option.

Developing and Testing Nuclear Weapons. Asked to specify the extent to which Pakistan should develop nuclear weapons, almost all advocates of weaponization (96 percent) called for the development of a nuclear arsenal capable of striking only India. An insignificant minority (1 percent) supported the development of a nuclear arsenal capable of striking all nuclear powers. A small number of nuclear advocates (3 percent) believed that Pakistan should develop all components but not actually assemble any nuclear weapons.

Over half (52 percent) of all respondents disapproved of a test to develop Pakistan's nuclear capability, including 64 percent of official policy supporters and 80 percent of nuclear opponents. Among nuclear advocates, however, 73 percent approved of such a test. If India were to conduct a second test, however, the number of respondents favoring a Pakistani nuclear test would increase significantly, with 73 percent of all respondents supporting such a test. Nonetheless, 27 percent said they would still disapprove of a nuclear test in these circumstances, including 32 percent of official policy supporters.

The Potential Impact of Sanctions. The influence of economic sanctions as either a motivating factor to justify the development of a nuclear arsenal or as a disincentive to weaponize appeared minimal. Not a single nuclear advocate or supporter of official policy felt that threats of economic sanctions would justify the development of nuclear weapons. Similarly, all nuclear advocates and supporters of official policy discounted the threat of international sanctions as a reason for the renunciation of nuclear weapons. A small number of supporters of official policy (2 percent), cited increased international pressure on Pakistan's domestic politics as a factor that would predispose them toward the development of nuclear weapons.

The Possible Use of Nuclear Weapons. Ninety-eight percent of all respondents—nuclear opponents, nuclear advocates, and supporters of official policy—felt that nuclear weapons could be used if India "were to attack Pakistan across the international border." Seventy-seven percent were also of the opinion that Pakistan could use nuclear weapons if India intervened militarily across Kashmir's Line of Control. No one would favor the use of nuclear weapons if another major Islamic state were threatened or in the event of military intervention by a U.S.-led coalition of countries. Only 1 percent of all respondents believed that nuclear weapons could be used accidentally. This is an extraordinary finding, given the lack of effective command and control systems in the Pakistani nuclear program (examined in chapters 3 and 5). The apparent disbelief in the possibility of accidental use is a reflection of the lack of understanding and knowledge about the nature of nuclear weapons systems among Pakistani elites.

Respondents seem to have a cavalier attitude about the actual use of nuclear weapons. Only 1 percent of those surveyed felt that nuclear weapons could never be used. There was no major difference in the opinion of all three groups on the use of nuclear weapons in the event of an Indian attack across the international border, though nuclear opponents (89 percent) were less likely than supporters of official policy (99 percent) or nuclear advocates (98 percent) to favor the use of nuclear weapons under such circumstances. Nuclear advocates scored higher (81 percent) than official policy supporters (77 percent) in their belief that nuclear weapons could be used if India intervened militarily across Kashmir's Line of Control. Nuclear opponents were the least supportive of the three groups of the use of nuclear weapons in such a scenario, but even among them, more than half (56 percent) believed that use in such circumstances was possible.

Views on Arms Control Issues. Official policy regarding the Nuclear Nonproliferation Treaty has consistently equated Pakistani acceptance of the treaty with Indian accession. This stand was largely reflected in the survey. There was very little support among respondents, whether official policy supporters, nuclear advocates, or nuclear opponents, for Pakistan's unilateral accession to the NPT. Among supporters of official policy and nuclear advocates (94 percent of the sample), no one favored unilaterally signing the treaty. Even among nuclear opponents, only 15 percent supported unilateral accession. On the other hand, 95 percent of those supporting government policy and even 91 percent of those favoring weaponization would support Pakistan's signing the NPT on the condition that India also signed the treaty. In the case of nuclear opponents, 76 percent would agree to a treaty-bound Pakistani renunciation of nuclear weapons if both Pakistan and India bilaterally signed the NPT.

There was also strong support among all respondents, including nuclear advocates, for global disarmament. While only 25 percent of official policy supporters and 18 percent of nuclear advocates cited a "global ban on testing and a time-bound plan for global disarmament" as a factor that would permit Pakistan to renounce the nuclear option, 97 percent of all respondents expressed total or partial support for an international agreement eliminating nuclear weapons. Sixty-one percent of all respondents "totally" supported such a treaty, while 36 percent supported it "to some extent." The degree of total support for nuclear abolition was especially high among backers of official policy, 71 percent of whom totally supported and another 27 percent partially supported such an agreement. Not surprisingly, 98 percent of nuclear opponents expressed total support. Even among nuclear advocates, 37 percent expressed total support, while 58 percent expressed some support.

There was remarkable optimism about the prospects of such a treaty. Ninety-one percent believed that an abolition agreement would be signed within the next five or ten years. Only two percent believed that such a treaty would never materialize. More than half of all official policy supporters (54 percent) believed that such a treaty would be signed within the next five years. Another 39 percent believed that it would be signed within ten years, while only 2 percent felt it would never be signed. Among nuclear advocates, 45 percent believed that the treaty would be signed within five years. Another 44 percent thought that a ten-year time frame was realistic, while only 3 percent discounted the signing of such an agreement. Nuclear opponents were the most optimistic of the three groups, with 76 percent believing that such a treaty would be concluded in five years, while no one thought that such a treaty was infeasible.

These findings are important since they portend a considerable degree of certainty that threshold states such as Pakistan and India would agree, in the foreseeable future, to cooperate with the international community to abolish all nuclear weapons. Since such cooperation would be dependent on a future resolution of Pakistan's differences with India and vice versa, this finding also suggests that Pakistan's educated elites have some optimism about an Indo-Pakistani reconciliation in the future.

Implications

The survey's findings demonstrate a high level of elite support for the official nuclear policy of ambiguity, and an acceptance of official justifications for the nuclear option. The perceived Indian threat is clearly the dominant factor in Pakistani elite perceptions of nuclear weapons policy. Support for the nuclear option is, therefore, likely to remain strong until tangible moves are undertaken toward regional peace and a reduction of tensions with India.

While public support for a nuclear weapons program is considerable, the salience of the nuclear issue is low. Pakistan's educated elites place far more emphasis on domestic concerns. Threats to internal security such as economic instability, underdevelopment, and ethnic tensions are perceived as more immediate and pressing than perceived or potential threats from external sources. It would seem logical to assume that socioeconomic reforms or political restructuring would be considered more important than the acquisition of a military capability to counter external threats.

Yet despite these pressing internal concerns, a majority of Pakistan's educated elite still regards the retention of nuclear capability of considerable importance, demonstrating the influence of official rhetoric on elite perceptions. The absence of information on nuclear issues is of particular importance in this context, since a number of the preferences and judgments reached by the respondents are based on insufficient knowledge. The fact that an overwhelming majority believed that nuclear weapons could be used in a future conflict in India is an obvious example. Another is the belief that the threat or imposition of international sanctions should be irrelevant to nuclear decision making. In both cases, the apparent disregard for consequences seems to reflect a serious lack of understanding.

Pakistani elites also fail to recognize how the country's de facto nuclear status weakens Pakistan's credibility and standing in international diplomacy. Nuclear nonproliferation is a widely shared norm in the international system, notwithstanding the many inconsistencies of the nuclear weapons states, and Pakistan's ambiguous stance outside of that international consensus entails diplomatic costs. India has suffered most in this regard and has found itself increasingly isolated in international fora, as evidenced by the September 1996 vote on the CTBT in the UN General Assembly, when India stood alone with Bhutan and Libya against the entire international community. Pakistan weakens its standing by pairing itself with India in rejecting the NPT and CTBT, thereby losing opportunities to advance the country's diplomatic interests. This in turn has limited Pakistan's ability to win greater international support for its major foreign policy objectives, most importantly in Kashmir, where the Pakistani position hinges on an internationalization of the dispute. A failure to acknowledge or even debate these consequences has deprived the country of the opportunity to consider alternative diplomatic options.

Any shift in elite opinion toward denuclearization will, above all, require an informed internal debate in Pakistan. There is an urgent need for greater public education to assess the existing and potential costs of nuclear weapons policy. To a considerable extent, a tangible opening and widening of the debate on the nuclear option will depend on the overall political environment. Discernible changes in elite perceptions are far more likely to occur within the context of a functioning democratic order. This will require greater governmental transparency in policy making and freedom of expression on nuclear issues.

Enhanced international support and assistance in democratizing both Pakistani society and the nuclear debate can play a positive role in influencing elite perceptions and preferences. On the other hand, continued support and encouragement for the Pakistani armed forces, as embodied in the Brown and Harkin-Warner amendments, is unlikely to advance democratization and may impede the consideration of alternative security paradigms. The policy of inducements for denuclearization, as recommended by the task force of the Council on Foreign Relations, is a sound one,[39] but the emphasis should be on incentives that encourage democratization and empower civil society, not on measures that strengthen the forces of repression. Similarly, the international community could play a positive role, through bilateral and multilateral initiatives, to facilitate dialogue between the Pakistani and Indian governments to defuse existing tensions. Policymakers on both sides should be encouraged to resolve their differences through the use of diplomacy rather than the use or the threat of use of force. Any move toward regional peace and a reduction of tensions with India would reduce the dangers posed by nuclear proliferation in South Asia and enhance public support for denuclearization.

Notes

1. Of these nonnuclear states, more than twenty are technologically capable of going nuclear but have shown no interest in developing weapons programs. See Michael McGwire, "Nuclear Weapons Revisited: Is There a Future for Nuclear Weapons?" *International Affairs* 17, no. 2 (April 1994): 220.

2. According to Mr. Khan, Pakistan possessed "elements which, if put together, would become a device." R. Jeffrey Smith, "Pakistan Official Affirms Capacity for Nuclear Device," *Washington Post*, 7 February 1992, A18.

3. Quoted in Leonard S. Spector and Jacqueline R. Smith, *Nuclear Ambitions: The Spread of Nuclear Weapons 1989–1990* (Boulder, Colo.: Westview Press, 1990), 107.

4. *Dawn* (Islamabad), 7 September 1997.

5. See dissenting comments of Leonard S. Spector in Council on Foreign Relations, *A New U.S. Policy Toward India and Pakistan* (New York: Council on Foreign Relations, 1997), 51–52.

6. Mark Hibbs, "U.S. Believes Khushab Still Cold, No Heavy Water Sold by China," *Nucleonics Week*, 3 July 1997; reprinted in *The Congressional Record*, 105th Cong., 1st Sess., 1997 (16 July 1997): S7556–7.

7. See remarks of Senator John Glenn, *The Congressional Record*, 105th Cong., 1st Sess., 1997 (16 July 1997): S7555–6; see also Marcus Warren, "Pakistan Nuclear Program at a 'Screwdriver Level,'" *The Washington Times*, 20 February 1996, A1.

8. *A New U.S. Policy*, 24–25.

9. See David Cortright, ed. *The Price of Peace: Incentives and International Conflict Prevention* (Lanham, Md.: Rowman and Littlefield, 1997).

10. *A New U.S. Policy*, 36.

11. Ibid., 23.

12. *New York Times*, 3 February 1997, A6.

13. The most vocal and assertive advocates of nuclear deterrence include former foreign secretaries Agha Shahi and Abdul Sattar. According to Mr. Shahi, the "military value (of nuclear weapons) derives from the political weight of a nuclear armory and the definition this gives to political stability between the concerned nations and blocs," while Mr. Sattar believes that the "attainment of nuclear capabilities by Pakistan and India has helped promote peace and stability and prevented dangers of war despite aggravation of tensions at times." Agha Shahi, "Future of the NPT," *Defence Journal* 21, nos. 1 and 2 (1995): 33; Abdul Sattar, "Reducing Nuclear Dangers in South Asia," *Defence Journal* 21, nos. 1 and 2 (1995): 24.

14. David Fischer, *Stopping the Spread of Nuclear Weapons: The Past and the Prospects* (London: Routledge, 1992), 97.

15. Ashok Kapur, *Pakistan's Nuclear Development* (London: Croom Helm, 1987), 15.

16. In his most quoted statement, Bhutto said, "If India developed an atomic bomb, we too will develop one 'even if we have to eat grass or leaves or to remain hungry' because there is no conventional alternative to the atomic bomb." Quoted in Zafar Iqbal Cheema, "Pakistan's Nuclear Policies: Attitudes and Posture," in *Nuclear Non-Proliferation in India and Pakistan: South Asian Perspectives*, edited by P.R. Chari, Pervaiz Iqbal Cheema, and Iftekharuzzaman (New Delhi: Monohar, 1996), 105.

17. The proposed Pakistani nonproliferation regime focused on the establishment of a nuclear weapon-free zone in South Asia. Stephen P. Cohen, "Policy Implications," in *Nuclear Proliferation in South Asia*, edited by Stephen P. Cohen (Boulder, Colo.: Westview Press, 1991), 359.

18. Fischer, *Stopping the Spread of Nuclear Weapons*, 77–78.

19. Kapur, *Pakistan's Nuclear Development*, 182–83.

20. Spector and Smith, *Nuclear Ambitions*, 96.

21. Leonard S. Spector, *The Spread of Nuclear Weapons 1987–88: The Undeclared Bomb* (Cambridge, Mass.: Ballinger, 1988), 129.

22. In his testimony to Congress in 1992, Robert Gates, CIA director, suggested that the F-16s supplied to Pakistan could be put to such use. Cameron Binkley, "Pakistan's Ballistic Missile Development: The Sword of Islam?" in *The International Missile Bazaar*, edited by William C. Potter and Harlan W. Jenkins (Boulder, Colo.: Westview Press, 1994), 88.

23. George H. Quester, "Nuclear Pakistan and Nuclear India: Stable Deterrent or Proliferation Challenge?" *Military Technology* 17, no. 10 (October 1993): 67.

24. *Congressional Quarterly*, 9 April 1994, 851.

25. *Dawn* (Islamabad), 18 July 1997; *The News* (Islamabad), 24 July 1997.

26. Remarks of Senator Tom Harkin, *The Congressional Record*, 16 July 1997, S7551.

27. John J. Schulz, "Riding the Nuclear Tiger: The Search for Security in South Asia," *Arms Control Today* 23, no. 5 (June 1993): 6.

28. McGwire, "Nuclear Weapons Revisited," 213.

29. Tehmina Mahmood, "Nuclear Non-Proliferation Treaty (NPT): Pakistan and India," *Pakistan Horizon* 48, no. 3 (July 1995): 98. Dr. Abdul Qadeer Khan, the head of Pakistan's nuclear laboratories, states, "In the absence of India signing the NPT or a bilateral agreement with Pakistan, Pakistan cannot sign the NPT and cannot allow itself to be subjected to nuclear blackmail." Dr. A.Q. Khan, "The Spread of Nuclear Weapons among Nations: Militarization or Development," in *Nuclear War, Nuclear Proliferation and their Consequences,* edited by Sadruddin Aga Khan (Oxford: Claredon Press, 1986), 425.

30. *The Muslim* (Islamabad), 4 August 1996.

31. Statement of the PML-N information secretary, Mushahid Hussain. *Dawn* (Islamabad), 23 July 1996.

32. *The Muslim* (Islamabad), 6 August 1996.

33. *Dawn* (Islamabad), 14 September 1996.

34. According to the official, "We have protected our interests and Pakistan is not being targeted today by anybody." Pakistan's chief delegate, Munir Akram, had told the UN General Assembly that Pakistan supported the resolution since it endorsed the objectives of a test ban treaty, but could not sign due to its concerns about the policies of its "nuclear militant" neighbor. *Dawn* (Islamabad), 11 September 1996 and 12 September 1996.

35. Ibid., 12 September 1996.

36. According to Foreign Minister Agha Shahi, for example, since India has conducted a nuclear test, signing the CTBT will not make any difference to it. But Pakistan has not tested its nuclear program so far; and CTBT accession would prevent such a test, closing an option that has so far prevented and contained Indian aggression. See the editorial, "Nuclear Program—A Guarantee for National Security," *Nawa-i-Waqt,* 6 December 1996.

37. It is difficult for nuclear opponents to express their dissent with Pakistan's nuclear policy when policymakers and their supporters take the stand, for example, that "Anybody opposed to the Kahuta (Ultracentrifuge) Enrichment Plant must be treated as a traitor of Pakistan . . . ." See the editorial in *The Muslim,* Islamabad (then under the editorship of Mushahid Hussain, one of the most prominent supporters of the nuclear weapons program). Cited in Cheema, "Pakistan's Nuclear Policies," 118.

38. In its election manifesto for the February 1997 elections, the Baluchistan National Party categorically rejected nuclear, chemical, and biological weapons. *Dawn* (Islamabad), 7 December 1996.

39. *A New U.S. Policy,* 32.

2

Deliberate Nuclear Ambiguity

By Zahid Hussain

The nuclear and missile arms race now underway in South Asia has made the region one of the most dangerous in the world and a potential nuclear flash point. India and Pakistan have fought three wars—in 1948, 1965, and 1971, and on three other occasions—in 1984, 1987, and 1990—have come perilously close to the brink of renewed conflagration. Many analysts believe that another armed conflict between the two countries could lead to nuclear war. Testifying before the U.S. Congress in 1993, the director of the Central Intelligence Agency, James Woolsey, warned that the arms race between India and Pakistan represented "the most probable prospect for the future use . . . of nuclear weapons." The CIA chief reported that both countries have the capacity to build nuclear weapons and could assemble an atomic bomb at short notice.[1]

Confirmation of Pakistan's nuclear capability has come from its highest officials. In February 1992, Pakistan's foreign secretary, Shaharyar Khan, told an interviewer for the *Washington Post* that his country had developed sufficient components to assemble at least one nuclear bomb.[2] Two years later, in August 1994, then former prime minister Nawaz Sharif, declared at a public rally at Neelabhat in Azad (or free) Kashmir, that Pakistan possessed the atomic bomb.[3] Most recently, Prime Minister Sharif declared at a Defense Day rally on 7 September 1997 that "Pakistan's nuclear capability is now an established fact."[4] These statements and others like them from high-level officials confirm what Western intelligence agencies have long suspected. Despite the ambiguity shrouding its clandestine nuclear program, Pakistan has achieved nuclear weapons capability.

This chapter sets the context of Pakistan's nuclear policy and traces the development of the program since the 1970s. It describes the evolution of the nuclear program and explains why the present policy of maintaining a de facto nuclear weapons capability within the rubric of ambiguity is likely to continue.

The Regional Context: Capabilities and Policies

Estimates of the scale of Pakistan's nuclear program are shrouded in secrecy and uncertainty. By January 1994, the U.S. administration believed that Pakistan had enough bomb-grade material for six to eight nuclear weapons and that it could produce additional highly enriched uranium for one or two bombs a year. The highly authoritative study *Plutonium and Highly Enriched Uranium 1996: World Inventories, Capabilities, and Policies* estimates that "at the end of 1991 Pakistan had enough material for eight to thirteen nuclear weapons."[5] Although Pakistan reportedly capped its uranium enrichment program in 1989 and in 1991, it could reactivate the process within a short period of time. Independent verification of the enrichment capping has not been possible, since the nuclear facilities involved are not subject to international nonproliferation safeguards. More recently, press accounts have reported Pakistan's purchase of 5,000 specialized ring magnets from China for centrifuges at the Kahuta nuclear plant that could be used for enriching uranium. Despite the supposed cap, Pakistan is believed to have continued production of low-enriched uranium at its Kahuta plant. This low-enriched uranium could be transformed into weapons-grade uranium within a matter of months. According to estimates in *Plutonium and Highly Enriched Uranium: World Inventories, Capabilities, and Policies,* between 225 and 420 kilograms of weapons-grade uranium could be produced within thirteen months.[6] This translates into a capability to produce an additional eleven to twenty-one bombs. In total, Pakistan has the potential for an arsenal of nineteen to thirty-four nuclear weapons.[7] Meanwhile Islamabad has invested substantial resources in the construction of a plutonium production reactor and reprocessing facility at Khushab on the Jhelum River in Punjab. Pakistan has also acquired midrange M-11 missiles from China and has developed its own *Hatf* indigenous ballistic missile program.[8]

While Pakistan's controversial nuclear weapons program has evoked strong international concern, it provides many Pakistanis a sense of security and is seen as a deterrent against yet another war with its bigger and more powerful neighbor. With the persisting tension between India and Pakistan over Kashmir, the nuclear option has become an important ingredient of Pakistan's military strategy. Nuclear weapons are seen as vital for maintaining Pakistan's sovereignty. The Kroc Institute poll found 100 percent of those interviewed citing threats from India as the main reason why Pakistan should develop nuclear weapons. Pakistani military officials believe that the nuclear option acts as an effective deterrent and can contribute to the fighting ability of the army.[9] Public opinion supports this view. According to the Kroc survey, 98 percent of respondents felt that nuclear weapons could be used if India "were about to attack Pakistan."

Seventy-seven percent believed that Pakistan could use nuclear weapons if India attacked across the Line of Control in Kashmir.

India's enormous conventional military advantage over Pakistan and its development of nuclear weapons and ballistic missile systems provide ample grounds for Pakistani concerns and impetus to Islamabad's drive toward nuclearization. India conducted a nuclear test in 1974 and has maintained a large-scale and active nuclear program for decades. India's nuclear estate is almost entirely outside international safeguards. American officials believe that India has enough fissile material for sixty to eighty nuclear weapons.[10] New Delhi has also tested and deployed a short-range ballistic missile, the *Prithvi*, and a medium-range missile, the *Agni*, is under active development.

Pakistan's nuclear weapons program is closely intertwined with that of India. The prospects for denuclearization in the two countries are also linked. Pakistan has expressed a willingness to sign the Nuclear Nonproliferation Treaty (NPT) and the Comprehensive Test Ban Treaty (CTBT) provided India does the same. Most Pakistanis support the mutual elimination of all nuclear weapons in South Asia. This thinking is reflected in the Kroc Institute survey. Ninety-one percent of all respondents favored Pakistan signing the NPT along with India. Islamabad has consistently proposed undertaking simultaneous steps toward making South Asia a nuclear-free zone. India has rejected such proposals, asserting that disarmament must be on a global rather than regional basis.

There are also some hard-liners, however, who advocate Pakistan's openly going nuclear regardless of the Indian position. One-third of the respondents in the Kroc Institute study favored weaponization of the nuclear option. As tensions between the two countries over Kashmir have heightened, there has been growing pressure from the pronuclear lobby to shed ambiguity regarding the nuclear option. Nuclear hawks, like former generals Aslam Beg, Khalid Mahmood Arif, and Hamid Gul, favor Pakistan openly becoming a nuclear weapons state. They contend that only by declaring itself a nuclear power can Pakistan hope to negotiate peace and nonproliferation with India. "Pakistan should have a nuclear weapon. And if we have it we should demonstrate it at the right time," maintains General Arif, former vice chief of army staff under military dictator General Zia ul-Haq.[11] Arif also argues that if both India and Pakistan become nuclear powers, this will create mutual deterrence. The pro-bomb lobby maintains that on two occasions in recent years war between India and Pakistan was averted because of the nuclear factor.[12]

Moderate Pakistani intellectuals reject these arguments. They contend that by shedding ambiguity and becoming a nuclear power Islamabad would further isolate itself in the international community and jeopardize its security. The moderates are also skeptical of the view that the possession of nuclear weapons would provide a viable deterrent. Pervez Hoodbhoy argues that a few crude nuclear devices cannot safeguard Pakistan's security or even act as an effective deterrent against foreign aggression. Hoodbhoy and others also express the fear that nuclear weapons in the hands of adventuresome rulers could lead to a conflagration resulting in incalculable devastation. "If full-scale war should break out between Pakistan and India, there is a definite possibility that nuclear weapons would be used even though both sides recognize that it means mutual annihilation. Hence the argument that the atomic bomb can bring peace to the subcontinent is a false and highly dangerous one," maintains Hoodbhoy.[13]

The Emergence of the Bomb Program

Pakistan launched its nuclear program more than two decades ago when former president Zulfiqar Ali Bhutto announced his plans to develop atomic weapons at a secret meeting of scientists and civil and military officials in Pakistan's southern city of Multan in 1972, just months after the country had suffered a humiliating defeat in its war with India. Pakistan's decision to acquire a nuclear device was driven both by fears of Indian domination and a desire for prominence in the Islamic world. India's nuclear test explosion in May 1974 gave further impetus to Pakistan's plan for nuclearization. India's demonstration of its nuclear capability reinforced a sense of insecurity in a defeated nation. The two countries had fought three wars since their independence in 1947 and the military superiority of India was fully illustrated in the 1971 war. Against this backdrop Pakistan's nuclear program appeared to counter India's substantial conventional superiority and its newly acquired nuclear capability.[14]

Even before these developments then foreign minister Zulfiqar Ali Bhutto declared in 1966 that if India made a nuclear bomb Pakistan would follow suite. "Even if Pakistanis have to eat grass we will make the bomb," Mr. Bhutto asserted in an oft-quoted statement.[15] Bhutto had urged consideration of a military nuclear program while minister for Fuel, Power, and Natural Resources in the 1960s, but the priorities of the government of President and Field Marshal Ayub Khan focused on the resumption of Pakistan's special security relationship with the United States, and the desire to regain preferential access to Western conventional arms, which had been disrupted by the imposition of a U.S. embargo on military assistance and sales to Pakistan during the 1965 war.

Bhutto's assumption of the presidency and the dismemberment of Pakistan in the 1971 war drove home the realization of Pakistan's military vulnerability, transforming Pakistan's nuclear program, which had hitherto focused on civilian energy production, into one with a substantial military component. The 1973 oil crisis played a role in the evolution of Pakistan's nuclear program as well. The crisis not only caused a quadrupling of oil prices, but led to the realization that alternative means of energy were imperative for the country's security. According to Tahir-Kheli, the 1973 crisis also changed U.S. perceptions of the role of Pakistan. "The U.S. began to subscribe to an apocalyptic vision of the world held hostage by a number of newly important but unstable countries that might even become armed with nuclear weapons, if not developed indigenously then acquired through surrogates. Since the majority in the above category lacked the necessary infrastructure to build a credible nuclear program, Pakistan was seen by Washington as the missing link in the chain for the acquisition of nuclear weapons by these countries." Though certainly not a motivation for Pakistan's weapons program, this theme was used by Bhutto to extract concessions and capital from the United States and the Arab states respectively.[16]

When the Indian nuclear test occurred in 1974, therefore, momentum was already building for a more active military nuclear program. President Bhutto seized the opportunity presented by New Delhi to press ahead with the weapons program. Security concerns were the primary but not the sole factor in Pakistan's decision to develop nuclear weapons. Bhutto's vision of an "Islamic bomb" also fueled Islamabad's nuclear ambition. "We know that Israel and South Africa have full nuclear capability. The Christian, Jewish, and Hindu civilizations have this capability. The Islamic civilization was without it, but that situation was about to change," wrote Mr. Bhutto from his death row prison cell in 1978 prior to his execution.[17] The Pakistani leader believed that nuclear capability would provide Pakistan a leading role in the Islamic world.

Although initially invoked by Bhutto, the "Islamic bomb" concept has little or no relevance to current Pakistani policy and public thinking on nuclear issues. The Kroc Institute poll found no support among educated elites for the idea of Pakistan using its nuclear capability as a means of defending Islamic civilization. When nuclear advocates were asked why Pakistan should develop nuclear weapons, none of the 290 respondents cited protecting the Islamic world as a reason. Almost no one in Pakistan today believes the nuclear option has meaning beyond meeting the threat from India.

Initially, Pakistan intended to pursue both the plutonium and uranium enrichment routes to nuclear capability. Mr. Bhutto in 1974 reached an agreement with France for the supply of a reprocessing plant for extracting plutonium from the spent fuel of a power reactor. But Pakistan's bid to acquire a reprocessing plant, which seemed unnecessary for its small civil nuclear program, sent alarm bells ringing in the international community. Although the reprocessing facility was supposed to be placed under International Atomic Energy Agency safeguards, the plant would have allowed Pakistan to accumulate plutonium which it did not need for its one small, natural uranium-fueled reactor, but which could be of obvious use for a weapons program.[18]

Pakistan's move to acquire a nuclear reprocessing plant evoked serious concern within the U.S. administration. In 1976 Secretary of State Henry Kissinger was dispatched to Islamabad and later to Paris in a bid to halt the reprocessing deal. The U.S. Congress also adopted legislation to prevent the spread of nuclear weapons capability. In 1976 Congress adopted the Glenn-Symington amendment as part of the International Security Assistance and Arms Export Control Act. The amendment prohibited economic and military assistance to any country transferring nuclear materials, equipment, or technology. Aid could continue in spite of nuclear trade if the president certified that suspending assistance would adversely affect the interests of the U.S. and that the country in question was not developing nuclear weapons.[19] Congress also passed the Nuclear Nonproliferation Act in 1978. This act limited the authority of the Department of Energy to make peaceful nuclear exports by requiring each export to be licenced by the Nuclear Regulatory Commission and approved by the State Department.[20] Aid to Pakistan was cut off in 1977 at the initiative of the White House rather than through the Glenn-Symington amendment as part of the Carter administration's more aggressive stance against nuclear proliferation.[21] In August 1977 France acceded to growing nonproliferation pressures and agreed to suspend the delivery of the nuclear reprocessing plant to Pakistan. Bhutto later acknowledged the importance of the reprocessing plant in Pakistan's endeavor to develop nuclear weapons. "Pakistan was on the threshold of full nuclear capability. All we needed was the nuclear reprocessing plant," he declared.[22]

The overthrow of Mr. Bhutto in July 1977 and his subsequent execution by the military regime of General Zia ul-Haq did not affect Pakistan's nuclear program. General Zia's military junta continued the weapons project despite France's refusal to provide the nuclear reprocessing plant, largely through pursuit of the uranium enrichment path to nuclear weapons. As early as 1975, Pakistan began clandestinely to acquire hardware and technology for ultrahigh-speed centrifuges.[23] Through smuggling and black market channels, Islamabad obtained the hardware for building an enrichment plant in Kahuta near Rawalpindi. Islamabad reportedly built an elaborate secret network in the West for procuring uranium centrifuge and enrichment information.[24] Most of the equipment was acquired from Western European countries. From 1977 to 1980 Pakistan reportedly smuggled an entire plant for converting uranium powder into uranium hexafluoride, the gas-fired material used as feed for the Kahuta plant.[25] Dr. Abdul Qadeer Khan, a German-trained metallurgist who had worked at a Dutch engineering firm (whose parent company operated a centrifuge enrichment plant at Almelo, the Netherlands) was the key figure in developing the Kahuta project. Dutch government investigations suggest that Dr. Khan was responsible for smuggling out the gas centrifuge equipment as well as design information for German and Dutch centrifuges from the Almelo plant.[26] Dr. Khan settled down in Pakistan in 1976 to direct the Kahuta project. The plant was separated from the Pakistan Atomic Energy Commission and placed under direct military command. The Kahuta plant began operation in the 1980s, but it faced serious difficulties in the initial period and could not make significant progress toward enrichment. In response, according to a U.S. State Department memo, Pakistan began to seek technical help from China.[27] In recent years, as support from the West has dwindled, Beijing has become an increasingly important source of materials and technology for Pakistan's nuclear program.

Pakistan Achieves Nuclear Weapons Capability

The profound geopolitical changes that swept the region in the late 1970s, following the communist revolution and Soviet military invasion in neighboring Afghanistan, made Pakistan a crucial frontline state for the West. Alarmed by the Soviet invasion and eager to obtain Pakistani cooperation in mobilizing resistance to perceived Soviet expansionism, the United States lifted its ban on economic and military assistance to Pakistan and exempted the country from the nonproliferation provisions of U.S. law. By the 1980s Pakistan became one of the largest recipients of U.S. military and economic assistance. From 1982 to 1990 Washington provided Islamabad $5.4 billion in mostly military aid.[28] Most observers agree that after the Soviet invasion of Afghanistan, Washington needed Islamabad more than Pakistan needed the U.S. The Reagan administration decided to shut its eyes to Pakistan's nuclear program, which had earlier caused serious strains in Pakistan-U.S. relations. General Zia fully exploited Pakistan's emerging geostrategic importance to the West and accelerated the country's nuclear program.

According to a former senior official in General Zia's military regime who had been associated with the nuclear program from its inception, "by 1983 Pakistan had achieved nuclear capability and could have gone in for a test explosion, but General Zia missed the opportunity." This source argues that, given Pakistan's strategic position vis-à-vis Afghanistan at that time, a nuclear test would have provoked little international reaction.[29] Nevertheless, Pakistan's nuclear weapons program continued to make progress, and there is strong evidence to suggest that by the end of 1984, Pakistan had, through indigenous efforts, crossed the "red line" in uranium enrichment to more than 5 percent U235. That was the period when Pakistan feared an imminent attack from Mrs. Indira Gandhi's government in India. The threat of war led to an acceleration in Pakistan's nuclear program.[30]

In an interview in February 1984 for *Nawa-i-Waqt*, a national Urdu language daily, Dr. Khan declared that Pakistan was on the verge of achieving nuclear capability.[31] This was the first time that the head of Pakistan's nuclear program spoke publicly about the country's nuclear status. Some reports suggest that the interview was a deliberate leak to warn India that in the event of aggression, Pakistan could respond with nuclear weapons. General Zia subsequently confirmed Dr. Khan's part of the statement, but emphasized that Pakistan had only produced low-enriched, non-weapons-grade material.[32]

Since Pakistani policymakers were, however, well aware of the dangers of flouting Pakistan's nuclear capability, the official nuclear policy continued to rest on two platforms—the acquisition of a nuclear weapons capability, shrouded under the cover of ambiguity, and ostensible support for nonproliferation. In accordance with these policy guidelines, Pakistani policymakers continued to strengthen and expand Pakistan's nuclear infrastructure. At the same time, countless offers were put forward at international fora, as well as bilaterally to the Indian government, as proof of Pakistan's support for nonproliferation. These offers were, however, made conditional on a bilateral Pakistani and Indian renunciation of nuclear weapons capability. These included bilateral accession to the NPT; simultaneous Pakistani and Indian acceptance of full-scope IAEA safeguards; bilateral inspection of each other's nuclear facilities; and a bilateral or regional test ban treaty.[33]

These offers did not endanger Pakistan's nuclear ambitions since Pakistani authorities had correctly assessed that the Indian response would be negative. India had no interest in rolling back its nuclear weapons program. Pakistan's military regained a measure of domestic legitimacy as the guardians of the country's security while the negative Indian response reinforced public distrust of Indian motives. In the international arena, moreover, some of Pakistan's more ambitious nonproliferation proposals also won it a degree of credibility. Yet there was official concern about an adverse American response, especially since the U.S. was once again a major source of armament and economic assistance to the military regime.

Pakistan's progress in the nuclear field had alarmed officials in Washington. The U.S. Congress passed the Pressler amendment in 1985, requiring sanctions against Pakistan unless the president certified that Islamabad was not developing nuclear weapons. The Reagan administration warned

Islamabad of "grave consequences" if it crossed the 5 percent enrichment threshold.[34] General Zia's regime assured Washington that Pakistan would not cross the "red line," but evidence indicates that Pakistan in fact continued to develop its program. In their book, *The Spread of Nuclear Weapons 1989–90: Nuclear Ambitions*, Leonard Spector and Jacqueline Smith identify 1985 as a watershed in Pakistan's nuclear program. That was the year when Pakistan developed weapons-grade uranium enrichment capability. Spector and Smith assert that President Reagan was aware of this development but chose not to challenge Pakistani leaders on the issue. The administration invoked the waiver provisions of the Pressler amendment by annually certifying, contrary to accumulating evidence, that Pakistan was not developing nuclear weapons. "Thus the United States acquiesced in Pakistan's decision to move toward production of weapons-grade uranium," write Spector and Smith.[35]

U.S. intelligence concluded in 1986 that Kahuta had acquired nominal capability sufficient to produce enough weapons-grade material to build several nuclear bombs per year.[36] During this time Pakistan began constructing a second uranium enrichment program near Golra.[37] Meanwhile, a series of articles in the American press, quoting U.S. administration officials, reported that Pakistan had either acquired the capacity to build nuclear weapons or was on the verge of this capability. One report suggested that Pakistan could build the bomb at short notice by just assembling the components.[38] In March 1988 a report published in the *New York Times* quoted senior U.S. government sources as stating that Pakistan had accumulated enough highly enriched uranium for four to six nuclear weapons. It also said that Pakistan's weapon was based on a Chinese design and was more advanced than the first U.S. nuclear device.[39] Nonetheless, President Reagan continued to certify that Pakistan did not possess nuclear weapons capability, thereby allowing the continuation of U.S. aid. Confirmation of Pakistan's nuclear developments was provided a few years later by Pakistan's former chief of army staff, General Mirza Aslam Beg, who said in a 1994 interview: "By 1987, before my appointment as vice chief of army staff, Pakistan had acquired full nuclear capability."[40]

In March 1987, Dr. A.Q. Khan gave a controversial interview to the Indian journalist Kuldip Nayyar in which he boasted that the CIA's claim that Pakistan possessed the nuclear bomb was correct. The interview was simultaneously published in the *London Observer* and in Indian newspapers. Dr. Khan later retracted the statement, further entrenching the policy of nuclear ambiguity. Meanwhile in an interview with *Time* magazine in March 1987, General Zia repeated Dr. Khan's claim: "Pakistan has the capability of building the bomb . . . whenever it wishes."[41]

Both General Zia and Dr. Khan in their statements maintained a deliberate ambiguity about the country's actual nuclear weapons status. Nevertheless it was quite evident that Pakistan had made significant progress in its weapons program. This was the period when relations between India and Pakistan sunk to a very low ebb. Operation Brasstacks, a major Indian military exercise near the Pakistani border, resulted in massive troop mobilizations in both countries, as the threat of yet another war loomed large over the South Asian subcontinent. Some reports suggest that the interviews by General Zia and Dr. Khan were aimed at sounding a warning to India that Pakistan was capable of assembling a nuclear device in the event of war.[42]

The interviews of General Zia and Dr. Khan in 1987, like the earlier claim by Dr. Khan in February 1984, appear to have been deliberate efforts to threaten India with the specter of nuclear war, to use Pakistan's emerging nuclear weapons capability as a deterrent against possible Indian military aggression. A similar intent may have motivated Nawaz Sharif's August 1994 assertion of Pakistani nuclear capability during his visit to Kashmir: to use nuclear capability as a shield to protect Pakistan's interests in the disputed territory. In effect, this is a policy of deterrence by rhetoric, or put more bluntly, nuclear bluffing. Although the nuclear program remains shrouded in ambiguity, it is made real as an instrument of declaratory policy. Pakistan's nuclear weapons potential has thus become a stick that is used to threaten India during times of military crisis. As noted earlier, Pakistani leaders believe that this policy has been successful in deterring Indian military ambitions. Nuclear bluffing is a dangerous game, however, for there is always the risk that the opponent will call the bluff, in which case Pakistani leaders would face a grim choice: accepting humiliation and defeat, or launching potentially suicidal nuclear strikes.

Maintaining the Bomb

The death of General Zia ul-Haq in August 1988 and Pakistan's subsequent return to democracy did not bring significant change in the country's nuclear weapons program. Pakistan had acquired the status of a de facto nuclear state by the time a civilian government was installed. Under the new civilian administration, Pakistan's nuclear program continued to be run by the military and the president. Prime Minister Benazir Bhutto, the daughter of Zulfiqar Ali Bhutto, was kept out of the decision-making process. During her state visit to Washington in 1989, Prime Minister Bhutto assured the U.S. Congress that Pakistan neither possessed a nuclear weapon nor intended to build one. Bhutto was reportedly shocked when she was told by U.S. intelligence officials during her visit about the actual status of Pakistan's nuclear program.[43] That the highest elected official had no control or even knowledge of the nuclear weapons program was a sad commentary on the state of civil-military relations and Pakistani democracy.

In 1989 President George Bush warned Pakistan that its nuclear program should not advance beyond its existing level. In response, Pakistan capped its uranium enrichment. According to Robert Oakley, former U.S. ambassador to Pakistan, President Bush wrote letters to Pakistani leaders in the fall of 1989 urging them to freeze the country's nuclear program. Oakley maintained that Pakistan later in the same year informed Washington that it had followed U.S. advice and had capped its uranium enrichment program.[44] General Aslam Beg later confirmed that the capping decision was taken jointly by the ruling troika comprising the president, the prime minister, and the army chief. General Beg maintained that the capping did not affect Pakistan's nuclear program as it had already achieved nuclear weapons capability.

Pakistan accelerated its nuclear program once again in 1990, however, as tensions between India and Pakistan mounted over Kashmir. According to reports, Prime Minister Benazir Bhutto lost what little influence she had over Pakistan's nuclear program during that period. The decision to accelerate the enrichment program was reportedly taken by President Ghulam Ishaq Khan and the chief of army staff, General Beg. Later, after her ouster from power, Benazir Bhutto maintained in an interview with the ABC television network that she was kept in the dark about the country's nuclear program.[45] Bhutto's statement clearly indicates that Pakistan's nuclear program is not controlled by the elected prime minister but operates autonomously under the military and, until recently, the president. According to some reports, no prime minister has ever been allowed to visit the nuclear facility in Kahuta.[46] The most important questions about the decision-making process on the development and the control of nuclear weapons are apparently beyond the reach of the elected government.

Following the ouster of Benazir Bhutto's government through an army-backed constitutional coup, Washington stopped all economic and military aid to Pakistan in August 1990, as President George Bush invoked the Pressler amendment by refusing to certify that Islamabad did not posses nuclear weapons. The U.S. decision to impose sanctions on Pakistan came after the withdrawal of Soviet forces from Afghanistan and the collapse of the Soviet system in eastern Europe. Washington's action was largely due to the changed geopolitical situation. Pakistan had achieved nuclear weapons capability at least two years earlier, but Washington had ignored these developments because Islamabad was an important linchpin in the West's fight against communism. When this threat disappeared, Pakistan's help was no longer needed, and sanctions were imposed.

The stopping of American aid did not deter Pakistan from continuing its nuclear weapons program. In fact, by its action, Washington lost its leverage over Islamabad. The U.S. administration insisted that it would not consider the resumption of aid until Islamabad rolled back its nuclear weapons program. No government in Pakistan was in a position to fulfill that requirement for the sake of U.S. aid. President Ghulam Ishaq Khan, a stalwart supporter of the nuclear program, resisted American pressure. Across the political spectrum, political leaders were unanimous in rejecting U.S. pressure to abandon the nuclear program.

The Gulf War saw a burgeoning of anti-American sentiments in Pakistan and generated greater support within the military establishment for Pakistan to shed its ambiguity and go for a nuclear test. Army chief General Beg was the major advocate of an overt nuclear policy, urging that Pakistan develop a viable nuclear option as part of its defense strategy. The early end of the Gulf War and the victory of U.S.-led allied forces, however, created a sharp division in Pakistan's establishment. Prime Minister Nawaz Sharif adopted a moderate position on the nuclear issue. The enrichment program was again capped. Sharif's soft-pedaling of the nuclear issue was clearly indicated in an interview with *New York Times* correspondent Barbara Crossette in June 1991, when Nawaz Sharif declared that he wanted to take a more flexible position but was constrained by certain factors, by which he meant the hard-line faction in the military.[47] That same week Sharif proposed a conference of five nations to discuss an agreement on South Asian regional nonproliferation. He faced strong resistance from the army chief and other hawkish generals, however. In a letter to Nawaz Sharif in July 1991, General Beg warned him of the army's concern and urged him to take a clear and firm line on the issue.[48] General Beg's retirement in August 1991 not only brought relief to the Sharif government but also a positive response in Washington. Following General Beg's departure, a thaw developed in relations between the United States and Pakistan. The fundamental situation did not change much, however, as Islamabad firmly refused to accept Washington's demand for rolling back its nuclear weapons program.

Notwithstanding his flexibility, Nawaz Sharif remained under intense pressure to make public Pakistan's nuclear position. Perhaps because of this pressure, the prime minister instructed his foreign secretary, Shaharyar Khan, to declare Pakistan's nuclear status while on a visit to the United States. Mr. Khan's statement in the *Washington Post* in early 1992 was the first time that the Pakistani government officially unveiled its nuclear weapons position. As noted earlier, such statements are not only declarations of military capability but diplomatic gestures intended to send a message to other states. In this case the intended recipient of the message was not only India but the United States as well. Pakistan firmly signaled its determination to maintain and press ahead with its nuclear program, notwithstanding U.S. pressures. The declaration had the added political purpose of shoring up Nawaz Sharif's nationalist and patriotic credentials at home, and diverting attention from mounting criticisms over his government's inability to address Pakistan's pressing social and economic problems.

Future Options: Maintaining Deliberate Ambiguity

Until the 1980s, there had been a general consensus among the decision makers for maintaining ambiguity regarding Pakistan's nuclear status. But following the cutoff of U.S. aid and the mass uprising in Indian Kashmir in 1990, pressure mounted from the nuclear hawks to announce Pakistan's position as a nuclear power. Hawks, like former vice chief of army staff General Khalid Mahmood Arif and former foreign minister Agha Shahi, maintain that by declaring itself a nuclear state, Pakistan will have the status of a nuclear power. Shaharyar Khan's interview with the *Washington Post* and Nawaz Sharif's speech at Neelabhat in Azad Kashmir in 1994 seem to have been made under the influence of the pronuclear lobby.

Nonetheless, the Pakistani establishment generally has favored a continuation of the policy of deliberate ambiguity. This is evident in the results of the Kroc Institute poll, in which 61 percent of respondents supported the official policy of ambiguity, compared to 32 percent who favored a policy of overt weaponization. The preference for ambiguity is also evident in the direct linkage of Pakistan's nuclear policy with India's similar policy of nuclear ambiguity. Most Pakistani officials argue that this mutual ambiguity provides an effective deterrent and that a unilateral declaration of nuclear status would harm Islamabad's position.

Washington's hard-line approach in the early 1990s failed to restrain Pakistan from continuing its nuclear project. In fact the U.S. insistence that Pakistan roll back its weapons program created a deadlock in relations between the two countries and fueled a new stridency within the Pakistani military establishment. By 1993 many in Washington realized the futility of singling out Pakistan and imposing sanctions against it under the Pressler amendment. The Clinton administration began to develop a new U.S. policy of engagement rather than sanctions. During her visit to Pakistan in the first week of November 1993, U.S. assistant secretary of state for South Asian Affairs Robin Raphel discussed with Prime Minister Benazir Bhutto a new U.S. proposal to end the impasse. She told Pakistani leaders that the U.S. would consider a one-time waiver of the Pressler amendment and would supply military hardware Pakistan had paid for, but not received. In return, Islamabad would be asked to cap the dynamic part of its nuclear program—the enrichment of uranium beyond 5 percent U235—leaving untouched the de facto nuclear capability Pakistan had already acquired.[49] Raphel's visit was the first signal that the U.S. administration was prepared to review its hard-line policy on Pakistan's nuclear program. Later U.S. under secretary of state Strobe Talbott visited Islamabad and offered to lift the ban on the delivery of twenty-eight F-16 aircraft in return for Pakistan agreeing to freeze its uranium enrichment program and allowing intrusive verification of this freeze.[50] These proposals signified a pragmatic shift in U.S. policy on nuclear nonproliferation in South Asia. Washington no longer demanded a rollback of Pakistan's nuclear program, but was now seeking to freeze the status quo. What the Clinton administration hoped to achieve was a verifiable ban on the production of nuclear fissile material.

These changes in policy resulted in the Brown amendment to the 1996 Foreign Assistance Act, in which the U.S. Congress authorized the delivery of a $368 million package of military hardware that included three antisubmarine aircraft, twenty-eight surface-to-air missiles, 360 air-to-air missiles, and a range of artillery, equipment, and ammunition. The Brown amendment also allowed future economic and military aid. In 1997 the U.S. Senate adopted an additional measure, the Harkin-Warner amendment to the Foreign Operations Appropriations Act, which authorized military training assistance for the Pakistani armed forces and permitted Overseas Private Investment Corporation support for U.S. companies investing in Pakistan. No conditions or requirements were attached to these offers of assistance. In effect, these actions represented the abandonment of the previous U.S. policy of attempting to prevent Pakistani nuclear proliferation through sanctions. Explicit nonproliferation conditions were dropped, replaced by a hope that improved relations between Washington and Islamabad would encourage Pakistani leaders to show restraint in their nuclear and military policies.

For their part Pakistani leaders have maintained a firm stance against any concessions in return for the more flexible U.S. policy. American hopes for a capping or rollback of Pakistan's nuclear program have not been realized. Pakistani administrations have repeatedly insisted that a unilateral and verifiable capping of the nuclear program is unacceptable. "If we are unilaterally pressed for capping, it will be discriminatory and Pakistan will not agree to it," asserted Prime Minister Benazir Bhutto.[51] Chief of army staff General Abdul Waheed, during his visit to Washington in April 1994, also declared: "We cannot barter away our national security for a few pieces of military hardware."[52] As the Brown amendment was being approved by Congress in 1995, a parliamentary committee in Islamabad criticized Washington's "policy of discrimination" and concluded "we cannot barter away our nuclear capabilities for the resumption of American aid."[53] Barely a month after the passage of the Harkin-Warner amendment, Prime Minister Nawaz Sharif called on the U.S. to stop pressuring Pakistan on the nuclear issue, stating, "We consider this issue behind us, and the Pakistani nation does not want to discuss it."[54] Scarred by the previous shifts in U.S. policy, and fiercely protective of their military prerogatives, Pakistani political leaders remain wary of Washington's intentions and determined to maintain an autonomous nuclear weapons capability. Pakistan's tough position has essentially stalled the new U.S. strategy of engagement.

It is evident that in the present environment of conflict in South Asia no government in Pakistan is likely to agree to a unilateral freezing of its nuclear program. The findings of the Kroc Institute survey show that public opinion is not in favor of renouncing the nuclear option, certainly not unilaterally. Nuclear weapons are seen as a vital guarantee of security, not simply a matter of national prestige. The poll shows that a majority of Pakistanis would support the suspension of the nuclear weapons program, but only if India followed suit. Because the security threat seems to have increased over the past few years, with the heightening of tensions over Kashmir, Pakistani support for the nuclear weapons program has remained solid and even hardened. The decline of India's support for arms control and its own hardening of nuclear attitudes has contributed to Pakistani obstinacy and made it more difficult for any administration in Islamabad to consider unilateral accession to the NPT or the CTBT. Pakistan has supported the NPT and CTBT but refuses to sign either until India does so.

Reducing the looming threat of nuclear conflagration in South Asia will require an easing of political tensions between Pakistan and India. The Kroc Institute poll shows that support for the nuclear option in Pakistan is linked to the perceived threat from India, and that an improvement in political relations between the two would increase support for denuclearization. The key to overcoming political animosities would be a settlement in Kashmir, with India and Pakistan indicating a willingness to renounce the nuclear option if such a settlement could be reached. The prospects of resolving the Kashmir dispute in the near term are remote, however, so other venues will be needed to create a conducive atmosphere for meaningful dialogue on issues related to conflict prevention. At this stage, it seems unlikely that the two countries will agree to any proposal for capping their nuclear programs. Perhaps through bilateral and multilateral talks, if the overall political atmosphere improves, some understanding on denuclearization could be reached. The support for global nuclear abolition and Indo-Pakistani mutual disarmament demonstrated by the findings of the Kroc Institute poll and other surveys provides some encouragement that the disastrous nuclear race in South Asia could be brought to an end.[55]

Notes

1. Mitchell Reiss, "South Asia and Nuclear Proliferation: A Future Unlike the Past?" *RUSI Journal* no. 138 (6 December 1993): 63.

2. According to Mr. Khan, Pakistan possessed "elements which, if put together, would become a device." R. Jeffrey Smith, "Pakistan Official Affirms Capacity for Nuclear Device," *Washington Post*, 7 February 1992, A18. See also John J. Schulz, "Riding the Nuclear Tiger: The Search for Security in South Asia," *Arms Control Today* 23, no. 5 (June 1993): 5.

3. Chris Smith, "Nuclear Dangers in South Asia," *CDS Bulletin of Arms Control* no. 16 (November 1994): 17.

4. "We Have Higher Things on Agenda: PM," *Dawn: The Internet Edition*, 7 September 1997, http://dawn.com/daily/19970907/top3.htm.

5. David Albright, Frans Berkhout, and William Walker, *Plutonium and Highly Enriched Uranium 1996: World Inventories, Capabilities, and Policies* (New York: SIPRI/Oxford University Press, 1997), 276.

6. Ibid., 278. Albright et al., estimate that, according to a U.S. official citing the Chinese design plan provided to Pakistan, Pakistan needs twenty kilograms of weapons-grade uranium for each bomb it builds.

7. R. Jeffrey Smith, "Proliferation Concerns May Delay U.S. Arms Shipment to Pakistan," *The Washington Post*, 15 February 1996, A23.

8. Zahid Hussain, "The Bomb Controversy," *Newsline* (November 1991): 26–27. See also Cameron Binkley, "Pakistan's Ballistic Missile Development: The Sword of Islam?" in *The International Missile Bazaar: The New Suppliers' Network*, edited by William C. Potter and Harlan W. Jencks (Boulder, Colo.: Westview Press, 1994), 81.

9. Chief of army staff General Aslam Beg stated in 1989 that "both the nuclear option and missiles act as deterrents and these in turn contribute to the total fighting ability of the army," while another senior military official declared,"We should detonate the bomb and let the world know that we are a nuclear power." Zahid Hussain, "The Bomb Controversy," 24.

10. Albright et al., *Plutonium and Highly Enriched Uranium 1996*, 269

11. Hussain, "The Bomb Controversy," 24.

12. Mushahid Hussain, "A Bomb for Security," *Newsline* (November 1991): 32.

13. Pervez Hoodbhoy, "Not by the Bomb," *Newsline* (November 1991): 34 (b).

14. Leonard S. Spector, *The Spread of Nuclear Weapons 1987/88: The Undeclared Bomb*, for Carnegie Endowment for International Peace (Cambridge, Mass.: Ballinger Publishing Company 1988), 120–21.

15. Quoted in Zafar Iqbal Cheema, "Pakistan's Nuclear Policies: Attitudes and Postures," in *Nuclear Non-Proliferation in India and Pakistan: South Asian Perspectives*, edited by P.R. Chari, Pervaiz Iqbal Cheema, and Iftekharuzzaman (New Delhi: Manohar, 1996), 10.

16. Shirin Tahir-Kheli, *The United States and Pakistan: The Evolution of an Influence Relationship* (New York: Praeger, 1982), 119.

17. Zulfikar Ali Bhutto, *If I Am Assassinated* (New Delhi: Vikas, 1979), 137–38.

18. Spector, *The Undeclared Bomb*, 121.

19. International Security Assistance and Arms Export Control Act, Title 22 (Foreign Relations and Intercourse, subchapter X: Nuclear Nonproliferation Controls), U.S. Code, sec. 2799aa.

20. Public Law 242, 95th Cong., 1st sess., (10 March 1978).

21. "Restrictions on Aid and Military Sales to Pakistan: 1977–1997," in Leonard S. Spector, *Tracking Nuclear Proliferation: 1996* (Carnegie Endowment for International Peace, Washington, D.C.).

22. Bhutto, *If I Am Assassinated*, 138.

23. Leonard S. Spector, *The Spread of Nuclear Weapons 1986–1987: Going Nuclear*, for Carnegie Endowment for International Peace (Cambridge, Mass.: Ballinger, 1987), 103.

24. David Albright, "India and Pakistan's Nuclear Arms Race: Out of the Closet But Not in the Street," *Arms Control Today* 23, no. 5 (June 1993): 14.

25. Spector, *Going Nuclear*, 103–04.

26. Albright et al., *Plutonium and Highly Enriched Uranium 1996*, 274.

27. Albright, "India and Pakistan's," 14.

28. *Congressional Quarterly*, 16 May 1992, 1352.

29. "The Bomb Controversy," 24.

30. Ibid., 25.

31. *Nawa-i-Waqt*, 10 February 1984. Cited in Leonard S. Spector and Jacqueline R. Smith, *The Spread of Nuclear Weapons 1989–90: Nuclear Ambitions*, for the Carnegie Endowment for International Peace (Boulder, Colo.: Westview Press, 1990), 92.

32. Leonard S. Spector, *The Spread of Nuclear Weapons 1985: The New Nuclear Nations*, for the Carnegie Endowment for International Peace (New York: Vintage Books, 1985), 118.

33. Ali Sarwar Naqvi, "Pakistan: Seeking Regional Peace and Progress in a Non-Nuclear South Asia," *Arms Control Today* 23, no. 5 (June 1993): 11.

34. Spector, *The Undeclared Bomb*, 127.

35. Spector and Smith, *Nuclear Ambitions*, 94.

36. Albright, "India and Pakistan's," 15.

37. Spector, *The Undeclared Bomb*, 141.

38. Ibid., 129.

39. Ibid., 142–43.

40. Zahid Hussain, "Whodunit," *Newsline* (April 1994): 30.

41. William R. Doerner, "Knocking at the Nuclear Door," *Time*, 30 March 1987, 42.

42. Hussain, "Whodunit," 25.

43. Christopher Smith, *The Topography of Conflict: Internal and External Security Issues in South Asia in 1993* (London: Brasseys, 1993), 300–301.

44. Hussain, "Whodunit," 30–31.

45. Hussain, "The Bomb Controversy," 26.

46. George Perkovich, "A Nuclear Third Way in South Asia," *Foreign Policy* no. 91 (Summer 1993): 90.

47. Barbara Crossette, "Pakistan Asks Talks on Atomic Spread," *New York Times*, 7 June 1991, A3.

48. Ibid.

49. Zahid Hussain,"Uncle Sam's New Bait," *Newsline* (April 1994): 30.

50. Ibid., 28.

51. Zahid Hussain, "Carrot Talk," *Newsline* (April 1994): 26.

52. Ibid.

53. "Pakistan Must Have Nuclear Option, Committee Says," *Reuters News Reports*, 21 July 1995.

54. *Dawn* (Islamabad), 16 August 1997.

55. In an earlier survey, conducted by *Newsline* in 1994, 64 percent of all respondents supported Indian and Pakistani mutual elimination of all nuclear weapons. *Newsline* (April 1994): 35.

3

Renouncing the Nuclear Option

by Zia Mian

Pakistan has now become a nuclear weapons state. Nowhere is this more evident than in its way of talking about its nuclear weapons without really talking about them. The United States and the Soviet Union referred to their atomic weapons innocuously as the "gadget" and the "article." In Pakistan, it is the "option." Lacking a nuclear bomb that it can name, the debate in Pakistan is only about this "option," or nuclear "capability." There is hardly even a mention of what the "option" is for, or what the "capability" is to do, except that it is somehow nuclear. From a moral standpoint there is little difference between a nuclear "option" and a nuclear weapon. Having a nuclear "option" means deciding you may want to commit mass murder at some time in the future and are preparing for it now. The intention is there from the moment the decision is made that committing such murder is an option. The actual killing only involves deciding when to do it.[1]

Using language as an anaesthetic, a way to deaden feeling about what is being proposed, Pakistanis refuse to confront the reality of nuclear weapons. This is what psychologist Robert Jay Lifton has called "nuclear numbing," the process by which "we domesticate these [nuclear] weapons in our language and attitudes. Rather than feel their malignant actuality, we render them benign."[2] Few societies would consider it acceptable to debate whether to kill children, or to use famine as a way of controlling population. When it comes to nuclear weapons, however, moral reasoning is dulled. The issue is whether it is right to have the power to kill hundreds of thousands of people, perhaps millions. But this is not how the nuclear choice is usually posed. From the very beginning of the nuclear age there has been a tendency to talk only in terms of abstract military strategies and notions of national security, rather than nuclear weapons and the people they are designed to kill.

Pakistan is believed to have developed simple nuclear weapons of the kind that were used more than fifty years ago against Hiroshima. In Hiroshima, one such bomb killed between 210,000 and 270,000 people, and destroyed more than 90 percent of the city.[3] Pakistan's "nuclear option" amounts to being prepared to do the same thing to one or more of India's major cities. How many cities could be destroyed is not known. At the present time, according to the U.S. State Department, Pakistan may have six to eight nuclear bombs.[4] Similar estimates have been made by others. The Russian Foreign Intelligence Service suggested that Pakistan has four to seven bombs, a senior Indian official told the Indian media that Pakistan may have nine bombs, and a recent independent study concluded that Pakistan may have enough nuclear weapons material for eight to thirteen bombs.[5]

The suffering that would follow if even one city were attacked is hard to imagine. An early estimate suggested that an attack on Bombay would instantly kill between 103,000 and 265,000 people, while 26,000 to 175,000 would die if Delhi were the target.[6] More recent estimates confirm the scale of the potential destruction, with 136,000 deaths in Bombay and more than 220,000 people injured, while in Delhi the toll would be 40,700 deaths and 66,900 injured.[7] The most recent estimate, based on the 1991 Indian Census, is that as many as 700,000 people would die in Bombay alone.[8] It hardly needs to be added that many more would die subsequently from the effects of radiation. Since almost half the population of India, like that of Pakistan, is under the age of fifteen, about half of all these deaths would be children.

Keeping the nuclear option open means maintaining the capability and willingness to kill hundreds of thousands or millions of innocent civilians. This is a fundamentally immoral position which should be rejected out of hand. Giving up the nuclear option means recognizing that no purpose can justify the terrible devastation and suffering that would result from the use of nuclear weapons. In relinquishing the so-called nuclear option, Pakistan can also move toward overcoming the environmental, economic, social, and security consequences which come with the pursuit of nuclear weapons.

Nuclear Weapons Cost Lives

Creating and maintaining a nuclear weapons program, even as an "option," and even one as small as Pakistan's, exacts more than a moral toll. There is increasing evidence from around the world that the production of nuclear weapons, from the mining of uranium to the disposal of long-lived radioactive waste, causes sickness and death.[9]

The first public evidence of the human and environmental damage resulting from Pakistan's nuclear program has already emerged. It is to be found in Dera Ghazi Khan, the site of Pakistan's first, and for a long time only, uranium mining and processing operation. Officially part of the Pakistan Atomic Energy Commission (PAEC), this site is where workers mined the uranium that went to Kahuta to make nuclear weapons. In 1996 some 500 workers at the plant went on strike, demanding "payment of compensation to the heirs of the employees [who] died during their duty or became handicap[ped], provision of all necessary safety measures both at the plant and at the site, sacking of the doctor and lady doctor of the PAEC dispensary, as due to their incompetence several employees lost their lives."[10]   The government's response was draconian: "Security guards of PAEC and other law enforcing agencies have besieged the colony and all installations. No one is being allowed to enter or come out of the area."[11]

The outbreak of a strike over health and safety at Dera Ghazi Khan should not be surprising. Uranium mining is fraught with risk. Unlike a laboratory where highly trained scientists handle tiny amounts of such dangerous material with relative safety, the mining and processing of uranium ore is on an industrial scale. Its labor-intensive character leads to large numbers of relatively unskilled workers being exposed to short- and long-term risks. Uranium mining leaves behind vast amounts of waste that can leach into the soil and ground water. The transport and processing of ore can generate uranium dust which if inhaled even in small quantities causes an additional health risk.

The dangers continue as the uranium is enriched at the Kahuta facility. This involves the use of highly corrosive and toxic chemicals that react violently with moisture in the air and are fatal if breathed. Once the uranium has been enriched, it leaves behind a radioactive, toxic, and corrosive waste. There is no information about health and safety conditions at the Kahuta plant, or how the waste is dealt with. A.Q. Khan, head of the uranium enrichment program, has claimed that it took just six years to get Kahuta up and running, a "record time" for such a complex project.[12] In the rush to deliver results, health and safety issues may have been given a low priority. This danger increases if those involved feel they are engaged in a vital national project.

The United States, which invented many of the processes and technologies used in making nuclear weapons, is still struggling to come to terms with the waste from its uranium enrichment program. A recent report claims that the giant steel cylinders containing waste gas produced by enrichment plants are so radioactive that even the rust that forms and then falls off the outside has to be treated as "dangerous waste." The cylinders, despite being over one-third of an inch thick have corroded, and "every time one leaks, as some have, it releases puffs of toxic gas and uranium that can end up in the ground water."[13]

Pakistan is now constructing a new nuclear reactor for producing plutonium which can also be used to make nuclear weapons. The Khushab reactor is located on the banks of the Jhelum river, less than 200 km from Islamabad.[14] It will burn uranium to produce plutonium. This will pose new environmental risks. If this reactor were to have an accident it could pollute the river with radioactivity and thus poison irrigation and drinking water drawn from it all the way downstream. Since the Jhelum flows into the Chenab river, and then into the Sutlej, before joining the Indus, almost the whole of Punjab and Sindh would be at risk from such an accident.

Before it can be used to make weapons, the plutonium produced by the reactor needs to be extracted from used reactor fuel. This is done by reprocessing, which generates large amounts of dangerous radioactive waste. The U.S. Department of Energy has estimated that reprocessing accounts for 85 percent of the radioactivity released in the nuclear weapons production process, 71 percent of the contaminated water and 33 percent of the contaminated solids.[15] These wastes are extremely dangerous and must be isolated from the environment for at least 1,000 years.

No one knows how many lives have been lost or irreparably damaged and what environmental contamination has occurred from the search for nuclear security. Perhaps those responsible for the nuclear program know, but they believe they are under no obligation to tell anyone. What is clear is that as long as Pakistan retains its nuclear weapons it will need to keep at least some of these sites open, and the hazards will persist. If, as seems possible, Pakistan increases the size of its nuclear program, additional sites will become part of the nuclear weapons complex, and more communities will be exposed to the dangers of radioactive waste.

The Economic and Social Burden

The purely financial cost of Pakistan's nuclear weapons program is similarly kept secret. Even estimating the cost is difficult. Part of the problem is disentangling the money spent on the nuclear weapons program from that spent on the Pakistan Atomic Energy Commission (at a rough estimate over 30 billion rupees, about $1 billion, since 1980). The links between the two programs are indisputable. A.Q. Khan has described how the uranium enrichment project at Kahuta was looked after by a board of senior civil servants whose job was "to coordinate the activities of our project and that of the PAEC."[16] Many of the nuclear scientists and engineers who work on the bomb program must have received their training through the PAEC, for where else could Kahuta have found its "seven thousand highly skilled and professional people, including more than two thousand Ph.D.s, M.Phils, M.S.s, M.Sc.s, B.E.s?" Such a connection is illegal. The PAEC is bound by its legal charter to work only on the peaceful uses of nuclear energy.

Because the PAEC budget has partially subsidized the nuclear weapons program, it has been estimated that Pakistan would need to spend only an additional $25 million a year (at 1979 prices) on uranium enrichment to build up its capacity to make nuclear weapons.[17] Since Kahuta has been in operation for more than twenty years, this suggests that making nuclear weapons material has cost over $1 billion in current prices (i.e., allowing for inflation).

The nuclear weapons program has cost more than this, however. The cost of the new plutonium producing reactor at Khushab needs to be included, and the cost of the heavy water plant to supply it, as well as the reprocessing plant that will extract the plutonium from the reactor fuel after it has been produced. It has been estimated that these kinds of facilities can cost $300 million in 1979 prices.[18] At current prices this comes to around $750 million. Putting these figures together suggests that Pakistan's nuclear weapons program has cost at least $2 billion so far. It may be worth noting that, according to a recent study, the United States spent some $4 trillion to develop, produce, deploy, operate, support, and control its nuclear forces over the past 50 years. The cost of developing and producing nuclear weapons alone in the U.S. is estimated at $375 billion.[19]

The cost to Pakistan of its nuclear weapons program as noted above is an underestimate since it is relies on how much capital these facilities would have commanded in countries possessing the indigenous scientific, technological, and industrial capability to do all the things that are required. Much of Pakistan's nuclear infrastructure, and especially its uranium enrichment program, has been assembled from imported components and materials, including tons of special steel used to make centrifuges. These have been purchased covertly, and no doubt at highly inflated prices. The added costs of corruption, which have become part of every deal in Pakistan, cannot even be guessed at since it is not clear who kept the accounts, or whether any accounts were even kept.

The development of Pakistan's nuclear weapons program has gone hand-in-hand with an increase in military spending. Since the mid-1980s, when Pakistan first claimed to have nuclear weapons, its military spending has increased more than threefold, and its armed forces have grown by 20 percent. The increase in military spending in Pakistan has meant a reduction in development spending. Military spending in the 1996 budget was set at Rs 131 billion (nearly $3.5 billion), an increase of 14 percent over the previous year and twice the military budget in 1990, which equaled the budget allocation for development, i.e., for building schools, hospitals, roads, etc., in that same year. Since then military spending has increasingly overtaken development spending. In 1997, Pakistan's defense expenditures were 125 percent greater than government allocations for education and health, with the military budget claiming nearly 27 percent of total government spending.[20] This trend marks a return to the period immediately after independence when military security was deliberately given priority over social development. The finance minister of Pakistan, in the very first budget speech, said, "I confess that the expenditure on defence is higher than would normally be justified for a young state like ours . . . (this was) money, some of which under better conditions should have been available for the social, industrial and economic development of the country."[21] Fifty years later it seems the "better conditions" have still not arrived.

The effects of persistently lower-than-necessary development spending are cumulative. Each generation that is deprived of decent health care, housing, education, and employment is less able to provide these for the generation that follows. The result is a spiral of underdevelopment. It is evident that this is the case in Pakistan, since the country has slipped on the United Nations Development Programme's index of the quality of life from number 120 in 1992, to 128 in 1995, to 139 in 1997.[22]

The impact that this has had on the social fabric of Pakistan is not hard to see. The uneven and unjust process of development that has been at work for decades has empowered the state rather than the citizenry. Almost every community has found itself pitted against the state at some time or another. The Bengalis, the Baluch, the Sindhis, the Mohajirs, all have fought for some kind of justice from the state. The current sectarian conflict, with Sunni militants at war against the Shia, is yet another expression of this struggle for the scarce resources left over once the state has taken its gargantuan share.

To begin creating the conditions for just development, massive reductions in military spending will be necessary. Such reductions cannot take place as long as India is treated as an absolute threat—a threat which no expense can be spared to fight, one that requires nothing less than a willingness to use nuclear weapons. It is only by engaging in nuclear disarmament that Pakistan can free itself of an obsession with national security at the expense of everything else and begin to repair the damage this has done to the social life of its people.

Creating Support for Nuclear Weapons

Despite all these arguments against retaining nuclear weapons, there is overwhelming support by elites for nuclear weapons in Pakistan. The

Kroc Institute poll shows that, taken as a whole, over 90 percent of the country's professional, intellectual, social, military, and policy-making elite favor having a nuclear weapons capability of some kind. This view is shared by a larger public. A 1996 Gallup Pakistan National Urban Survey poll interviewed people from a wide range of backgrounds and asked: "In your view should Pakistan build or not build nuclear weapons? Are you in favour of building them or opposed?" Overall, the results are very similar to those obtained in the Kroc Institute poll; 80 to 90 percent of respondents supported nuclear weapons to some extent, while less than

Table 1: Public Attitudes Toward Nuclear Weapons for the Last Decade (Figures are in percentages)

	1987	1989	1991	1996
Strongly Support	78	68	71	76
Mildly Support	10	15	14	8
Oppose	4	8	4	4
No Opinion	6	6	8	8

Source: Pakistani Public Opinion on Nuclear Issues, Gallup Pakistan, 1996

10 percent were opposed.[23] There is also evidence that this level of public support for nuclear weapons is long-standing. A comparison with Gallup polls conducted since 1987 shows that when asked, "Should Pakistan make nuclear weapons?" responses have not changed significantly for a decade.

Table 2: Access to Information on Nuclear Issues (Figures are in percentages)

	Nuclear Advocates	Supporters of Official Policy	Nuclear Opponents
Difficult to Get	51	52	17
Almost Impossible to Get	31	15	9

Source: Kroc Institute Poll

The Kroc Institute poll hints at an explanation of this massive and unchanging support for nuclear weapons. It shows that even among the elite, who have the greatest access to information about issues, there is a widespread sense that getting information about nuclear issues is a problem.

What is more significant, though, is the clear relationship the poll results show between how little information people feel they have about nuclear issues and how strongly they support nuclear weapons. Only 26 percent of nuclear opponents felt that access to information on nuclear issues was a problem. However, among those wishing to retain a "nuclear option," a far higher proportion, 67 percent, felt that access to information was a problem; a staggering 80 percent of those wanting to turn the "nuclear option" into full-fledged, ready-to-use nuclear weapons found it "difficult" or "almost impossible" to get information.

The level and resilience of support for nuclear weapons and the lack of knowledge that seems to go along with it are connected. The information machinery of the Pakistani state has labored to maintain this connection. For decades, India has been projected as an absolute and unremittingly hostile enemy, without scruple, willing to exploit every opportunity to undermine Pakistan. It is presented as the source of everything that goes wrong in Pakistan, the mysterious hand behind every untoward event. No other explanation is necessary anymore, no questions need be asked. India cannot be reasoned with, or even understood; it must be confronted with every means at Pakistan's disposal.

The indoctrination process can be found at work even in the education of children. In the National Social Studies curriculum for children in Class V (taught in all government schools at the age of 9) there is a section entitled "Islamic Republic of Pakistan." The text says that the child should be able to "acknowledge and identify forces that may be working against Pakistan." These forces are identified explicitly as "India's evil designs against Pakistan (The three wars with India)" and "The Kashmir problem." The child is also taught to be able to "demonstrate a desire to preserve the ideology, integrity and security of Pakistan."[24]

This is not an isolated part of the curriculum. Another section is entitled "Safety" through which children "will be able to understand the role of the defence forces of Pakistan." Understanding begins with "safety from rumour mongers who spread false news" and "safety from foreign invasions." The detailed activities set out for the children are "to learn exercise of civil defence," and "to stage drama signifying the evils of rumours." They are also expected to "collect the pictures of policemen, soldiers and national guards."

This kind of indoctrination lays the groundwork for manufacturing a national consensus in support of nuclear weapons. It is reinforced by repeated public declarations from all of the presidents, prime ministers, and military leaders of the past twenty-five years that Pakistan's "nuclear option" is vital to the "national interest." One former chief of army staff, General Mirza Aslam Beg, has declared that giving up Pakistan's "nuclear capability" would be tantamount to committing "national suicide," adding that any compromise on the nuclear program would be "nothing short of high treason" since it would amount to "signing our death warrant."[25] When things are presented in this way, it is evident that many people will conclude that the "nuclear option" is Pakistan's last and only hope.

At the same time (and not altogether surprisingly given the language of public figures like General Beg), nuclear weapons are turned into a source of pride. A.Q. Khan has been turned into a national public figure. He is everywhere—on television and in newspapers, giving interviews, making speeches, opening schools, running a university. In a 1996 multipage special newspaper supplement to celebrate twenty years of the uranium enrichment program and his role in it, he was shown to be shaking hands with the president, accompanied by a page of "commendations" from former presidents and prime ministers, foreign ministers, and chiefs of army staff, including then former prime minister Nawaz Sharif, who declared, "We salute the dedication of Dr. A.Q. Khan (a national hero) and all his team members for giving a sense of pride to our nation."[26] The darkest element in the manufacture of the nuclear consensus is the way that dissent is projected as treachery. One can see this is at work in the deliberate orchestration of hate by sections of the media against individuals and groups who argue against nuclear weapons. One example will suffice to show how the process works. There was a seminar organized by the Islamabad branch of the Pakistan-India People's Forum for Peace and Democracy in February 1996. This meeting was reported under banner headlines that said, "People's Forum Meeting: Ridiculous Speeches Poking Fun at Islam, Abusing Armed Forces." The speakers were reported as having made "provocative speeches against Islam, Pakistan and the armed forces." For the record, the supposed provocation was the opinion expressed by speakers that Pakistan should not become engaged in a nuclear or missile race against India.[27]

Subsequent newspaper reports led with headlines such as "Prime Minister has ordered an inquiry into speeches against Pakistan and Islam. Organisers of non-Governmental dialogues between India and Pakistan are not patriots. Cases should be instituted against them." Another blared, "Prime Minister has ordered an inquiry into the slander against armed forces. This is treason against the country." In both stories, senior politicians were quoted as having said that this was a case of treason. Others went further, arguing that if the government would not act to prosecute such traitors, people should take the law into their own hands.

While this response was extreme, it was by no means unique. By claiming to be the sole guardians of the national interest, a handful of institutions and individuals have taken it upon themselves to set the limits of debate. By controlling public discourse in this way they strengthen the voice of authority and reduce the democratic process to tinkering around on the margins. In such a situation, no real solutions to the profound problems confronting Pakistan can hope to be found. It is only by giving up nuclear weapons that space can be created for a fresh start, a space free from the institutions and ideas which have held the country hostage and led it into its present crisis.

Nuclear Weapons Are No Defense

Why does Pakistan have a nuclear capability? In keeping with the numb and dumb nuclear debate, the answer is: Pakistan has a nuclear option because India has a nuclear option. The Kroc Institute poll shows this very clearly. There is unanimity among nuclear advocates that Pakistan should have nuclear weapons because of the threat from India. Nearly all respondents saw a direct linkage between the nuclear weapons programs in the two countries. The source of this way of thinking is easy to find. Zulfiqar Ali Bhutto offered the first justification for Pakistan's nuclear program in 1965, with his famous (or infamous) statement that if India were to produce a bomb Pakistanis would eat grass to get one of their own. The same justification is offered now. General K.M. Arif, former vice chief of army staff, has argued that Pakistan needs nuclear weapons because of India's "demonstrated behavior . . . a country that enjoys numerical superiority in conventional weaponry, possesses a variety of missiles, and has a large, weapon oriented nuclear program. The nuclear threat posed to Pakistan's security . . . cannot be met by it with either the conventional means of defense or external security guarantees."[28]

In 1969 Bhutto went further in offering a justification for nuclear weapons. He said, "All wars of our age have become total wars and it will have to be assumed that a war waged against Pakistan is capable of becoming a total war. It would be dangerous to plan for less and our plan should, therefore, include a nuclear deterrent." Not having such a deterrent, Bhutto argued, would "only enable India to blackmail Pakistan with her nuclear advantage."[29] This idea of "nuclear blackmail" finds its contemporary echo in the former chairman of the Pakistan Atomic Energy Commission, Munir Ahmed Khan, who presided over the earliest phase of the nuclear weapons program: Pakistan's "nuclear option is meant as a defensive measure to forestall nuclear blackmail and hegemony of India."[30]

The phrase "nuclear blackmail" is a loaded term aimed at inducing a public response based on familiarity with the common usage of the term blackmail. If nuclear blackmail is taken to mean the threatened use of nuclear weapons by one state to prevent or compel action by an opposing state then there is a long history of attempts to use weapons in this way.[31] The U.S. and the Soviet Union employed this tactic numerous times, with the United States issuing such threats twenty times and the Soviet Union five or six times. The threats were made against each other as well as against other states. It was undoubtedly this experience of superpower nuclear threats during the cold war that led to the claim that Indian nuclear weapons could be used in a similar way against Pakistan. But it is one thing to make such a claim and another to show that these threats were actually of real significance. A detailed study of the cases of cold war "nuclear blackmail" between the U.S. and the Soviet Union concludes that these "attempts" were ambiguous in execution and uncertain in effect" and that "the advent of strategic parity after the 1960s coincided with, but does not seem to have caused, a reduced incidence of nuclear blackmail."[32] In other words, the experience of the superpowers suggests that nuclear weapons are of no special use in coercing an opposing state and do not offer protection against such threats. This means that the assumption behind Pakistan's nuclear policy, that an Indian nuclear threat can only be stopped by Pakistani nuclear weapons, is based on a misunderstanding of the historical record. In particular, this record suggests that if India were ever to make nuclear threats against Pakistan, it would do so regardless of whether Pakistan had its own nuclear weapons or not.

India has had the opportunity to make a nuclear threat against Pakistan since testing a nuclear weapon in May 1974. At that time Pakistan had no nuclear weapons. It was not until more than a dozen years later that Pakistan began to acquire a rudimentary nuclear capability.[33] At any time during this period, India had a nuclear advantage and could have threatened Pakistan, secure in the knowledge that Pakistan could not retaliate. There is no evidence that such threats were made. The alleged threat of possible nuclear blackmail thus seems highly speculative. Moreover, as noted above, nuclear weapons offer no defense against such an eventuality in any case.

If nuclear weapons do not offer meaningful protection against threats of blackmail, what is left for them to do? The usual answer is that nuclear weapons are supposed to deter nuclear attacks and so prevent nuclear war between nuclear-armed states. That this can be much more easily and reliably done by giving up nuclear weapons is lost in much of the literature on this subject. Stripped of its pseudo-strategic terminology, the argument for nuclear deterrence is based on the idea that political and military leaders, their senses sharpened by the fear of nuclear destruction, will realize which actions are likely to lead to war, and will act rationally and in time to stop this from happening. The concept of deterrence is based on the hope that terrible fear will produce wise decisions among fallible people operating under intense pressure.

The presumed validity of the doctrine of deterrence is based on the experience of the superpowers during the cold war. The absence of war between the United States and the Soviet Union is widely attributed to the fact that both sides possessed nuclear weapons. This assertion is impossible to prove. All that can be inferred logically is that the absence of war coincided with both sides having nuclear weapons. The absence of war could more plausibly be explained by the simple fact that neither side really wanted a war. It has been argued, very convincingly, that the experience of total war during World War II was so terrible (the Soviet Union suffered more than 25 million casualties) that each side was sufficiently motivated to prevent another major war.[34]

While there is uncertainty about the role of nuclear weapons in preventing war, there is no doubt about their role in raising the stakes of superpower conflict. The presence of nuclear weapons in the U.S.-Soviet confrontation meant that any misjudgement, any mistake, could be potentially fatal. Every crisis had the possibility of becoming the spark that could start a nuclear war. How great this possibility actually was is only now coming to light. General George Lee Butler, who until 1994 was commander in chief of the U.S. Strategic Command and thus in charge of all American nuclear weapons, has said that catastrophe was avoided during the 1962 Cuban Missile Crisis, "no thanks to deterrence, but only by the grace of God."[35]

Tragically, deterrence thinking has arrived in Pakistan. It has come in the form of half a dozen subspecies of standard deterrence, exotic creatures with names like existential deterrence, opaque deterrence, and recessed deterrence. There is no shortage of statements that nuclear weapons are now keeping the peace in South Asia. Fewer voices are asking, however, what kept the peace before Pakistan had nuclear weapons. If only Pakistan's nuclear weapons prevent war, why was there no war during the years India had a nuclear monopoly? Such questions are rarely asked, because the answer undermines both the magical role ascribed to nuclear weapons and the assumption of an absolute and unremitting Indian threat. Instead, many wish to see Pakistan increase the scale of its nuclear weapons program. The Kroc Institute poll shows that about one-third of those interviewed want to see Pakistan "develop" its nuclear weapons. This can only mean that they want to see nuclear weapons assembled, tested, and then deployed, ready for use. Believing in nuclear deterrence as a necessity and fearing that it does not yet exist, they want to try to create it or its appearance. In doing so, they choose to ignore the fact they are making Pakistan a more likely nuclear target. Indian hawks need to justify their country's nuclear weapons. They need an enemy that they can point to, someone they can "deter." The Kroc Institute poll conducted in India in 1995 showed that over half of those who want India to further weaponize its nuclear program see "threats from a nuclear Pakistan" as the primary justification.[36] If Pakistan gave up its nuclear weapons, the Indian hawks would be thrown into disarray. They would have no reason to point nuclear weapons at Pakistani cities. Pakistan would be safer.

From Conventional to Nuclear War

The other major argument for the nuclear option is that atomic capability can save Pakistan in the event of conventional war with India, either by ensuring victory or at least serving to prevent defeat. There are many voices now making the link between Pakistan's nuclear weapons and Indian conventional forces. Air chief marshal (retired) Zulfikar Ali Khan has said that Pakistan's nuclear weapons are a deterrent to "the overwhelming conventional military superiority that India has clearly achieved." Former prime minister Moeen Qureshi claimed that a nuclear deterrent was "essential" for Pakistan because of India's supremacy in conventional arms.[37] In her own rather indirect way Benazir Bhutto has said the same thing, claiming that "a South Asian nonproliferation regime

Table 3: India and Pakistan's Military Forces

	India	Pakistan
Active Armed Forces	1,145,000	587,000
Tanks	3,500	2,050
Artillery	4355	1820
Aircraft Carriers	2	0
Submarines	19	9
Destroyers and Frigates	24	11
Attack Helicopters	309	32
Combat Aircraft	846	434

Source: The Military Balance 1996/1997, Institute for International Strategic Studies, 1996

will not be durable until the threat of Indian conventional attack has been removed."[38]

Like other official justifications for Pakistan's nuclear weapons, these arguments have taken root among the elite. The Kroc Institute poll shows that 36 percent of those who support official policy felt that Pakistan would be justified in developing nuclear weapons if India increased its "conventional arms advantage." More indirectly, about half of those who support official policy and over two-thirds of nuclear advocates agreed that a reduction in India's "conventional arms advantage" should be a condition for Pakistan renouncing its nuclear weapons.

The problem is easy to see. India has nearly twice as many active military personnel as Pakistan. In the key areas of land forces and air power, India has nearly twice as many tanks, two and one-half times as many pieces of towed artillery, and nearly twice as many combat aircraft.

The imbalance has been created and maintained at great cost. A study of military spending by the two countries shows that from 1958 to 1973 Indian military spending seems to have triggered increasing Pakistani military spending, as Pakistan tried to keep up with India as best it could. From 1973 onward, however, Pakistan increased its military spending in an effort to close the gap, while India increased military spending to maintain a large conventional military superiority.[39] Pakistan's defense expenditure in 1996–97 was estimated at 7 percent of gross domestic product (GDP) and for the fiscal year 1997–98 at 7.09 percent of GDP.[40] Since 1973 India has spent nearly $30 billion on importing weapons, while at the same time developing its nuclear weapons.

It is claimed that a nuclear weapons program will help Pakistan reduce its massive defense expenditure, thus making scarce economic resources available for development. A Pakistani security expert recently claimed, for example, that "any major reduction . . . in Pakistan's defense expenditure," which is necessary to meet human development needs, "will only come if the defense establishment changes over from the current military policy of maintaining large, non-nuclear forces to small, well trained, non-conventional forces."[41] If Pakistan's military leaders are serious about using nuclear weapons as a deterrent against conventional attack, this means they are prepared to turn a conventional battle, like those fought by India and Pakistan in 1948, 1965, and 1971, into a nuclear war. Pakistan's refusal to accept a no first strike agreement with India is suggestive that Pakistan's armed forces are prepared to do just that. The Kroc Institute poll shows that such use of nuclear weapons would probably command public support. Nearly 80 percent of the supporters of official policy and of nuclear advocates agreed that Pakistan could use nuclear weapons "if India were to intervene militarily across Kashmir's Line of Control." Almost all of them think Pakistan could use nuclear weapons "if India were *about to attack* across the international border" [emphasis added].

What does it mean to consider using nuclear weapons first in such a situation? It means, first of all, being prepared to kill countless Indian civilians because of the failure of political and military leaders to prevent war. Certain horrible but inescapable conclusions follow. The first and obvious one is that hundreds of thousands if not millions of Indians would be killed. The second is that, in the words of retired general Mujib ur Rehman Khan, "Pakistan's first strike against India will bring the fury of India's atomic power on our heads and it will entail the devastation of Pakistan . . . The world will pronounce Pakistan's doom."[42] With a few nuclear weapons Pakistan cannot hope to destroy India's ability to retaliate. By using nuclear weapons against India, it will have invited the annihilation of Pakistan. This is clearly possible. India is estimated to have produced sufficient plutonium to make between sixty and eighty nuclear weapons.[43] Less than half that number would utterly destroy Pakistan.

Then there is geography to contend with. India's size means that any Pakistani military offensive could reach only a limited part of India. If Pakistan's armed forces use nuclear weapons, their choice of targets will be limited. In contrast, Pakistan is a compact country. Every part of it lies within the reach of Indian military forces. The destruction on both sides would be beyond description, but unlike war between nuclear superpowers—with their intercontinental ballistic missiles able to reach anywhere—the destruction would be not be mutual. India would survive, but Pakistan would cease to exist.

An inescapable dilemma confronts any possible decision to use Pakistan's nuclear weapons. General Khan has commented, "Will Pakistan resort to nuclear means at the fall of Lahore, or when a strategic area is about to be overrun? By the time we are in a position to take such a momentous decision, our present borders will have been pushed inwards towards the interior, putting us that much more at a disadvantage. At the same time, the Indians will have attained the necessary air superiority to have turned the scale of the conventional battle to their advantage. Under such adverse conditions, how do we launch this nuclear strike to stem India's military success?"[44]

This is no idle speculation. One recent analysis has suggested that for two decades the Indian air force has been determined in its efforts "to amass a strike capability that could be expected to involve attacks on Pakistan's nuclear delivery systems, especially its airbases."[45] Imagine, for example, if the Indian air force attacked the Sarghoda airfield, where Pakistan is supposed to keep its Chinese-made M-11 missiles, or a base where F-16s were waiting to be armed with nuclear weapons. Under such "adverse conditions" Pakistan's military leaders may be tempted to use nuclear weapons out of fear that they might lose them altogether.

Even if there is no planned first strike with nuclear weapons and nuclear weapons are not used intentionally, there is always the chance of their accidental use. This possibility has worried even former Pakistani chief of army staff, General Beg: "Pakistan and India may neither have the resources nor the capability to develop . . . a system for ensuring nuclear safeguards and security." As a consequence, an attack, he says, could "escalate to a nuclear level" where "there can be a real danger of nuclear accident and unauthorised use of nuclear weapons due to the absence of a fail-safe system."[46] In other words, nuclear weapons could be used accidentally, or by someone who was not supposed to be able to make the decision.

Any first use of nuclear weapons by Pakistan, whether as a planned first strike or as an inadvertent or accidental use, would likely lead to a retaliatory nuclear response from India. The only way to ensure against this risk is to remove nuclear weapons from Pakistan's military planning. It is only by not having them that there can be certainty that they will not be used. Renouncing the nuclear option means Pakistan has the double benefit of not having these weapons and not having them used against it. It will be neither nuclear executioner nor nuclear victim.

Nuclear Weapons Can Do Nothing For Kashmir

In the minds of Pakistan's elite, there is one last issue that is connected to the nuclear option. The Kroc Institute poll shows that the settlement of the Kashmir dispute with India is seen as the most important issue facing the country, and is linked closely to that of nuclear weapons. Approximately 70 percent of those who support government policy and 80 percent of nuclear advocates agreed that a final settlement with India on the Kashmir issue would allow Pakistan to renounce its nuclear weapons. Conversely, 77 percent of official policy supporters and 81 percent of nuclear advocates favored the actual use of nuclear weapons if India were to cross the Line of Control in Kashmir. But how can nuclear weapons play a role in the situation of the Kashmir dispute?

Much of what has happened in recent years in Kashmir can be understood by looking at the superpower confrontation during the cold war. Unable to resolve their conflict, but unwilling to risk direct warfare, the U.S. and the Soviet Union turned the world into a battleground. No place was too small, no issue too minor to contest. In Central America, Africa, and across Asia, proxy wars raged while nuclear weapons "served to discourage the process of escalation." A "tacit code of conduct" came into play about how to interfere. This code included "don't use your own forces against an adversary's ally or protectorate" and "don't paint the adversary into a corner so that he must choose between humiliation and escalation."[47] Pakistan has learned this lesson. Emboldened by a nuclear shield that makes it unable and unwilling to take the hard decisions that would be needed to settle this long-standing dispute, Pakistan indulges in aggressive diplomacy as well as proxy war against India.

India has deployed hundreds of thousands of soldiers and paramilitary forces to put down the movement for self-determination in Kashmir. The Pakistani state as well as religious parties based in Pakistan have intervened to provide support to sections of this movement. While the full extent of the support is unknown, the Kashmiri leader Yasin Malik has claimed that in addition to the 10,000 Kashmiri militants there are nearly 2,500 "guest" militants.[48] The consequence has been a "carefully calibrated war of proxy and subversion" that has left more than 40,000 Kashmiris dead, and many more wounded.[49] Kashmir's economy has been wrecked and an entire generation of Kashmiris has already been deprived of normal upbringing and education.

Given the two inconclusive wars between Pakistan and India over the status of Kashmir, in 1948 and 1965, what is the likelihood of war breaking out again over Kashmir? Eqbal Ahmad has argued that if Pakistan and India should go to war over Kashmir "neither Pakistan nor India is likely to win . . . If perchance a decisive outcome appeared likely, nuclear weapons shall surely enter the scene, resulting at best in an inconclusive cease-fire or, at worst, a continental holocaust. Military leaders in both countries share this estimation of the military balance."[50] While there are military reasons why war is unlikely, the fact is that in the event of war there will be enormous political pressures and nationalist passions pushing for a "decisive outcome," creating the possibility of "continental holocaust."

The way this pressure is likely to manifest itself was demonstrated during the last war with India. Former cabinet secretary Hasan Zaheer has described the path to war as he witnessed it in 1971:

> East Pakistan vaguely figured as a side issue; the psyche was to retrieve the fruits of victory of which the nation was deprived by Ayub's cease-fire in the 1965 war. Private cars and public vehicles and places were plastered with 'Crush India' stickers. The radio was blaring martial music exhorting people to be ready for jihad, interspersed with vulgar parodies of India film songs about the person of Mrs. Gandhi. The people—and they included the well-educated classes—had been carried away by the 'one Muslim equals ten Hindus' syndrome which had caught the imagination of even the professional soldier, who ought to have known better.

The impact of this was felt at the highest levels: "The emergency committee meeting on 29 November discussed the intelligence reports of the public criticism of the army as having neither the will nor the capacity to take action in the west."[51]

Zaheer identifies clearly the three reasons why all-out war was the outcome. "The decision to go for an all-out war was clearly not taken on purely military considerations. It was based on a mixture of fear of public wrath, false assumptions of intervention by friendly countries, and hurt egos from the failures of the previous eight months."[52] This kind of behavior was no aberration. It had happened in 1965 when Pakistan last had tried to "liberate" Kashmir. Air Marshal Nur Khan, who was then commander in chief of the Pakistan air force, has said: "It was almost unbelievable how a whole government could live in such a fool's paradise and bluff itself into thinking that this operation could be carried out successfully."[53]

Acquiring nuclear weapons has not helped Pakistan solve the Kashmir conflict. It has not been able to force a solution. The only way to do so would be through war, and that would be no solution. Giving up nuclear weapons need not mean giving up support for the movement for self-determination in Kashmir. After all, Pakistan supported this cause before it had nuclear weapons. Giving up nuclear weapons does mean abandoning the strategy of trying to hide behind a nuclear shield and "bleeding India through Kashmir." It means accepting that all Pakistan can do is help negotiate a settlement that the Kashmiris want.

Giving Up Nuclear Weapons

Fifty years ago, Pakistan's political leaders made a fateful choice. Newly partitioned and fearful of the future, they elevated military security above the well-being of the people. Their mistaken ideas of national security led to more than half of all central government spending being allocated to the military every year for the first twenty years. The consequences were a militarization of Pakistani society and its relations with India and a criminal neglect of people's needs. Twenty-five years later, Pakistan's political leaders were faced with another fateful choice. Partitioned again, with the same fears for the future, they put their trust in nuclear weapons. The consequences again were dismal. Military spending still consumes more than half of central government spending— once the massive debt repayments about which the government has no choice are subtracted. In the 1997–98 budget, 45 percent of net federal reserve receipts will go toward debt servicing.[54] Military security still has priority over the health, education, and shelter of the people.

It is worthwhile to reiterate the reasons why Pakistan should renounce its nuclear weapons before addressing the final question of how best to give them up. The first reason is ethical. Nuclear weapons are instruments specifically designed to commit indiscriminate mass murder. Hiding this reality behind the innocuous language of a "nuclear option" or "capa–bility" changes nothing. There is no justification for having or using such weapons, and whether other states have them or not is irrelevant. The intention and preparations to commit mass murder are simply immoral.

The second reason is that nuclear weapons allow the state to distort society. Public consent to nuclear immorality is manufactured by political and military leaders while the environmental and economic costs are ignored. The public is kept ignorant about the consequences of having nuclear weapons and a sense of hostility toward the enemy is promoted. Dissent is stifled and democratic debate is undermined.

The third reason is the least understood, because it is the most unexpected. Nuclear weapons offer no defense. They cannot defend against the possibility of nuclear blackmail, they cannot protect against defeat in war, and there is no guarantee that deterrence works. Against India's conventional forces, Pakistan's nuclear weapons offer only the prospect of deliberate first use, or accidental use. These could lead to Indian nuclear retaliation and the destruction of Pakistan.

A fourth reason why Pakistan should give up its nuclear weapons is that if Kashmir really is the major foreign and defense policy problem for Pakistan, nuclear weapons cannot help. They only encourage sections of the Pakistani state to believe there is now a shield behind which Pakistan can try to "bleed" India in Kashmir. This helps no one, and certainly not the Kashmiris. If Pakistan were prepared to go to war with India over Kashmir and to use nuclear weapons in such a war, the outcome would be no Pakistan, and probably no Kashmir.

Taken singly or together these reasons present the case why Pakistan should disarm. The only question is how? There are three options. Pakistan could renounce its nuclear weapons as part of an international agreement on nuclear disarmament, or as part of a bilateral process with India (as has been done by Argentina and Brazil), or it could unilaterally renounce these weapons (as South Africa has done).

There is unfortunately no immediate prospect of an international agreement to ban nuclear weapons. Fifty years have passed since the United Nations first called for such a ban, and it has been more than twenty-five years since the nuclear weapons states who signed the Nuclear Nonproliferation Treaty promised, as part of the treaty, that they would disarm.

There is equally no prospect of a bilateral agreement between India and Pakistan to renounce nuclear weapons. It is clear from New Delhi's refusal to sign the Comprehensive Nuclear Test Ban Treaty in 1996 that India sees an explicitly global dimension to its nuclear weapons. It has refused to sign the treaty in part because the United States and other nuclear weapons states can still develop and test nuclear weapons in laboratories and by using computers. The fact is that India is unlikely to give up its nuclear weapons even if Pakistan does. It is time that those wanting Pakistan to "keep the nuclear option open" realize this, and decide whether they want to support the indefinite maintenance of Pakistan's nuclear weapons.

The best and easiest way for Pakistan to disarm is to do so unilaterally. Unilateral actions do not leave Pakistan dependent on the wishes, intentions, or actions of India or any other state. By unilaterally disarming Pakistan would secure a new position in the international community. Choosing to renounce nuclear weapons because it's the right thing to do, rather than doing so under external pressure or as a result of internal collapse, would transform Pakistan's position in the outside world. The experience of South Africa is instructive here. Since it gave up its nuclear weapons unilaterally, South Africa has emerged as one of the key leaders of the Non-Aligned Movement at the UN and in other international fora. The benefits could include a more sympathetic international hearing for settling the Kashmir dispute. Most importantly, unilateral disarmament would be an act of self-empowerment. It would mean that educating Pakistan's children and providing health care, jobs, and homes to its people will no longer be held hostage and these areas could at last receive the priority they deserve.

Notes

1. John Finnis, Joseph M. Boyle, and Germain Grisez, *Nuclear Deterrence: Morality and Realism* (New York: Oxford University Press, 1987), 110–13.

2. Robert Jay Lifton and Richard Falk, *Indefensible Weapons: The Political and Psychological Case against Nuclearism* (New York: Basic Books, 1982), 106.

3. Nobuo Kusano, comp., *Atomic Bomb Injuries* (Tokyo: Tsukiji Shokan Company, 1995), 65.

4. Mitchell Reiss, *Bridled Ambition: Why Countries Constrain Their Nuclear Capabilities* (Washington, D.C.: Woodrow Wilson Center Press, 1995), 192.

5. David Albright, Frans Berkhout, William Walker, *Plutonium and Highly Enriched Uranium 1996: World Inventories, Capabilities and Policies* (New York: SIPRI, Oxford University Press, 1997), 277.

6. Zalmay Khalilzad, "Nuclear Proliferation and Stability in Southwest Asia," in *Strategies for Managing Nuclear Proliferation: Economic and Political Issues*, edited by Dagobert L. Brito, Michael D. Intriligator, Adele E. Wick (Lexington, Mass.: Lexington Books, 1983), 190.

7. S. R. Naim, "Aadhi Raat Ke Baad," in *Nuclear Proliferation in South Asia: The Prospects for Arms Control*, edited by Stephen P. Cohen (Boulder, Colo.: Westview Press, 1990), 48.

8. M.V. Ramana, "Effects of Nuclear Weapons: A Case Study of Bombay" (paper presented at the regional meeting of the International Physicians for the Pre-

vention of Nuclear War, New Delhi, February 1997).

9. Arjun Makhijani, Howard Hu, Katherine Yih, *Nuclear Wastelands: A Global Guide to Nuclear Weapons Production and its Health and Environmental Effects* (Cambridge, Mass.: MIT Press, 1995), 23–104.

10. *Dawn* (Islamabad), 23 October 1996.

11. Ibid.

12. A.Q. Khan, "Dr. A.Q. Khan Research Laboratories, Kahuta: Twenty Years of Excellence and National Service," *The Friday Times* (Islamabad), 5–11 September 1996, and *Dawn* (Islamabad), 31 July 1996.

13. M.L. Wald, "Danger from Uranium Waste Grows as Government Considers its Fate," *New York Times*, 25 March 1997.

14. *Dawn* (Islamabad), 7 March 1996.

15. U.S. Department of Energy, Office of Environmental Management, *Linking Legacies: Connecting the Cold war Nuclear Weapons Production Processes to their Environmental Consequences* (Washington, D.C., 1997), 6.

16. A.Q. Khan, "Dr. A.Q. Khan Research Laboratories."

17. T.W. Graham, "The Economics of Producing Nuclear Weapons in Nth Countries," in *Strategies for Managing Nuclear Proliferation: Economic and Political Issues*, edited by D.L. Brito, M.D. Intriligator, A.E. Wick, (Lexington, Mass.: Lexington, 1983), 12.

18. Ibid.

19. S.I. Schwartz, *The U.S. Nuclear Weapons Cost Study Project* (Washington, D.C.: Brookings Institution, 1997).

20. Aslam Sheikh, "Arms and People in South Asia," *The News* (Islamabad), 13 April 1997.

21. Cited in Zia Mian, "The Poverty of Security," in *Rethinking Security, Rethinking Development*, edited by N. Naqvi, (Islamabad: Sustainable Development Policy Institute, 1996), 113.

22. United Nations Development Programme, *Human Development Report 1997* (New York: Oxford University Press, 1997), 139.

23. Gallup, *Pakistani Public Opinion on Nuclear Issues*, Gallup Pakistan, 1996.

24. Zia Mian, "The Making Of The Pakistani Mind," *The News* (Islamabad), 6 November 1994.

25. General (ret.) Mirza Aslam Beg, "The Atomic Programme and the Political Ramblings," *Pakistan Times*, 11 December 1993.

26. A.Q. Khan, "Dr. A.Q. Khan Research Laboratories."

27. Zia Mian, "The Good, the Bad and the Ugly," *The News* (Islamabad), 18 February 1996.

28. Gen. (ret.) Khalid Mahmud Arif, "No Bargain on Nuclear Option," *Dawn* (Islamabad), 6 December 1994.

29. Quoted in A.Q. Khan, "Dr. A.Q. Khan Research Laboratories."

30. Munir Ahmed Khan, "Understanding Pakistan's Nuclear Plan," *The News* (Islamabad), 8 March 1995.

31. Richard K. Betts, *Nuclear Blackmail and Nuclear Balance* (Washington, D.C.: Brookings Institution, 1987).

32. Ibid, 227.

33. According to A.Q. Khan it was "on July 31, 1976, when the first real seeds of Pakistan's nuclear program were sown," and it took a further six years to "put

Pakistan on the nuclear map of the world." This first public claim of nuclear capability did not come until 1987. See Dr. A.Q. Khan, "Dr. A.Q. Khan Research Laboratories."

34. John Mueller, *Retreat from Doomsday: The Obsolescence of Major War* (New York: Basic Books, 1989).

35. George Butler, Speech at the Stimson Center, Washington, D.C., 8 January 1997.

36. David Cortright and Amitabh Mattoo, eds., *India and the Bomb: Public Opinion and Nuclear Options* (Notre Dame, Ind.: University of Notre Dame Press, 1996), 125.

37. Zia Mian, "Changing Nuclear Plans," *The News* (Islamabad), 12 March 1995.

38. Benazir Bhutto, "Pakistan's Foreign Policy," in *After The Cold war: Essays on the Emerging World Order*, edited by Keith Philip Lepor, (Austin, Tex.: University of Texas Press, 1997), 155.

39. R.E. Looney, "Budgetary Dilemmas in Pakistan: Costs and Benefits of Sustained Defense Expenditures," *Asian Survey*, (May 1994): 421.

40. Sheikh, "Arms and People."

41. Nasim Zehra, "Defense Budget 1997–98: Compulsion not Options," *The Nation*, (26 June 1997).

42. Lt. General Mujib ur Rehman Khan, "A False Sense of Security," in *Pakistan's Atomic Bomb and the Search for Security*, edited by Zia Mian (Lahore: Gautam Publishers, 1995), 35.

43. Albright et al., *Plutonium and Highly Enriched Uranium 1996*, 269.

44. Lt. General Mujib ur Rehman Khan, "A False Sense of Security," 36.

45. Eric Arnett, "Conventional Arms Transfers and Nuclear Stability in South Asia" (paper presented at the IXth International Summer Symposium on Science and World Affairs, Cornell University, Ithaca, N.Y., August 1997).

46. Zia Mian, "Fenced in by Fear," *The News* (Islamabad), 7 January 1995.

47. Kurt Gottfried, Bruce G. Blair, *Crisis Stability and Nuclear War* (New York: Oxford University Press, 1988), 279.

48. Gautam Navlakha, Rita Manchanda, and Tapan Bose, "Political Situation in Kashmir: Duped by Media and Government," *Economic and Political Weekly* (20 July 1996).

49. Eqbal Ahmad, "Confronting Reality in Kashmir," *Dawn* (Islamabad), 28 July 1996.

50. Ibid.

51. Hasan Zaheer, *The Separation of East Pakistan: the Rise and Realization of Bengali Muslim Nationalism* (New York: Oxford University Press, 1994), 358–59.

52. Ibid.

53. *The Herald* (Islamabad), September 1994.

54. M. Ziauddin, "Debt Servicing to Eat Up 45 Percent," *Dawn* (Islamabad), 14 June 1997.

4

Pakistan's Nuclear Future

by Pervez Hoodbhoy

This chapter speculates on possible future breakwaters against the rising nuclear tide in India and Pakistan. Given that the nuclear weapons programs of both countries are shrouded in secrecy, it is hazardous to guess where they might be one, two, or five decades from now. To do so requires an assessment of uncertain political, economic, and technological factors. At the political level one must understand why Pakistan presently seeks the bomb, and whether the intensity of this motivation is likely to change over time. Economics will determine how much Pakistan can continue to spend on its nuclear program, and technological factors will shape the range of available options as it moves beyond the present rudimentary stage of nuclear development. My conclusion is that Pakistan will continue to strive for a nuclear deterrent force, but that economic and technological weaknesses will impose increasingly more stringent, perhaps crippling, constraints on the growth of its nuclear program. It is therefore highly likely that Pakistan's nuclear program will cap itself even if political or military forces wish it to be otherwise.

In the latter part of this chapter, I outline policy options for an intentional capping of the nuclear program that could reduce nuclear tensions on the subcontinent. The stress is on the possible. To believe that Pakistan will, or can, give up nuclear weapons in the present circumstances is but a pipe dream, especially in light of the hardening of Indian nuclear attitudes over the last decade. These attitudes make it neither politically feasible nor desirable, given the various instabilities that would result, for Pakistan to unilaterally renounce nuclear weapons. It is noteworthy in this regard that only 6 percent of the Pakistani elites interviewed by the Kroc Institute poll supported the renunciation option. Even if complete denuclearization is not possible at the moment, it is nonetheless extremely important to search for solutions that limit the nuclear competition in South Asia. Both countries are desperately poor and cannot afford a full-blown arms race. In addition, the chances of miscalculation or accident leading to a nuclear war are by no means negligible, and make the search for a solution ever more urgent.

Why The Bomb?

The results of the Kroc Institute poll confirm the Indocentric basis of Pakistan's insecurity. Every single respondent saw India as the reason for Pakistan to seek nuclear weapons. This Indocentric reasoning goes something like this: India has never accepted the idea of Pakistan. India dismembered Pakistan in 1971 and exploded a nuclear device in 1974. It seeks to reduce all its neighbors to mere Bhutans. India is a military behemoth and a regional hegemon with a blue-water navy. The result of such thinking is a virtually unchallenged belief that Pakistan's security and survival lie in its preparing, as quickly as possible and as many as possible, the weapons of ultimate destruction.

The facts of India's military capabilities, even if rhetorically stated, are undeniable. However, they do not adequately explain why Pakistan so desperately seeks nuclear weapons. It is difficult to believe on rational grounds that the bomb is necessary because India seriously seeks to undo the partition of 1947. Although India would seek to humiliate Pakistan militarily in a war, physical occupation of Pakistani population centers by Indian troops is out of the question. The latter would be beyond the limits of India's power to execute for any length of time, as is evident from its never-ending difficulties as an occupying force in the tiny state of Kashmir. Thus, the bomb is not necessary to ensure the physical existence of Pakistan. Also not fully convincing are the appeals against India's burgeoning military power. Proximity to a larger, more powerful neighbor does not automatically drive every militarily weaker country in the world to seek a nuclear deterrent. Digging deeper reveals that the imperative for the Pakistani bomb has three other critically important elements that have generally received less attention than they deserve.

The first element is belief in the "nuclear shield" doctrine. This assumes that Pakistan can continue to provide support to Kashmiri militants struggling against Indian rule without fear of a retaliatory Indian invasion. Without this shield, argue nuclear proponents, there could be a large-scale Indian attack across the Line of Control or the international border, initiated out of frustration and a desire to punish Pakistan if the Indian army should suffer unacceptable losses in insurgent attacks.

In informal discussions, military leaders have indicated that a large-scale Indian attack could drive Pakistan to use nuclear weapons. The poll results show that public opinion is supportive of this position. Ninety-eight percent of those polled agreed that Pakistan could use nuclear weapons if India were to launch an attack across the Line of Control. Since Pakistan is an undeclared nuclear state, it has never enunciated a nuclear doctrine, and nuclear targeting has never been discussed. However, the general belief is that instead of "wasting" its handful of weapons against military formations, Pakistan would focus on high-value targets—Delhi, Bombay, and other Indian cities within the range of its delivery aircraft. The Indians are presumably not willing to pay this price, and so an invasion will have been deterred while preserving Pakistan's ability to influence the Kashmiri struggle. What is most interesting is that debate on nuclear doctrine has never gone beyond this rather elementary, simple-minded level. No military or civilian leader has ever indicated interest in discussing issues like decapitating strikes, survivability of the command and control system, accidental nuclear war, permissive action links (PALS), and so forth.

To be sure, Pakistan's initial quest for the bomb was not particularly with Kashmir in mind. Instead, it was spurred by India's 1974 test explosion at Pokhran, which followed in the wake of the 1971 Indo-Pakistani war. It was believed that India's atomic bombs had to be countered by Pakistan's atomic bombs. For more than a decade this was the focus of Pakistani thinking. But India's rapid advances in missile development and military technology gradually changed Pakistani attitudes into what they are today—a belief that Pakistan can deal with the Indian military colossus only if it has the protection of its undeclared nuclear arsenal. Only thus can it continue its support to Kashmiris and not have to worry about an invasion from across the border. This new rationale was articulated by a former director of Inter-Services Intelligence (ISI), who was later Pakistan's ambassador to Germany. "If," argues General Asad Durrani, "we were to make it clear that whatever nuclear deterrence we might have is primarily meant to deter the use of nuclear weapons from the other side, then by so saying we will fail to deter a conventional attack . . . ." Therefore, he reasons, the other side must be led to believe that "we are primed, almost desperate to use our nuclear capabilities when our national objectives are threatened, [as] for example, a major crackdown on [the] freedom movement in Kashmir . . . ."[1]

The "nuclear shield" logic is now a de facto element of Pakistani policy even if it has never been officially articulated. It derives additional justification from the claimed near-nuclear confrontation over Kashmir in May of 1990, the "Cuban Missile Crisis" of the subcontinent. Many Pakistani believers of nuclearization cite this as the nation's first exercise of its nuclear muscle, and offer it as proof of its power to deter. Although the facts seem to indicate that the alleged reports of nuclear movements were false, the belief that Pakistan's threat of nuclear devastation stopped Indian aggression dead in its tracks has become enshrined as an article of faith.

In the Pakistani view Kashmir is the unfinished business of partition. Without its accession to Pakistan the principles by which the Islamic state was created stand to be fundamentally violated. From the Indian perspective, the loss of Kashmir to Pakistan would amount to the unraveling of the state's fabric as a secular and multiethnic entity. These irreconcilable positions have provoked two wars between 1948 and 1965. In this tiny northern state, India maintains an army of nearly half a million, spends roughly $10 million a day, suffers or inflicts 10 to 15 casualties daily, and now has run out of all options but the iron fist.[2] Estimates of Kashmiri casualties range up to 50,000, according to the chief minister of Jammu and Kashmir, Farooq Abdullah, and the opposition Hurriyat Conference. An estimate of 55,000 to 60,000 deaths is given by Syed Nagic Gillani, secretary general of the Jammu and Kashmir Council for Human Rights.[3] Pakistani estimates put the number of Indian troops and paramilitary forces deployed in Jammu and Kashmir at approximately 600,000; according to Indian sources five divisions of the Indian army, 50,000 troops of the border security force, and 250,000 police personnel are deployed in Jammu and Kashmir.[4] Pakistan formally denies supporting the insurgency and says that it provides only moral support. It is widely believed, however, both in Pakistan and elsewhere, that there is a steady flow of weapons and militants across the border. This is the principal source of tensions to which nuclear weapons have added a new dimension.

How does the future look? Compromise on Kashmir does not appear to be in the cards in either country, and there is no substantial indication that the stalemate will be broken in years to come. The probable implication for the future is that the nuclear shield doctrine will become increasingly more attractive for Pakistan as the military asymmetry between the two countries shifts further to its disadvantage. The first two India-Pakistan wars resulted in a stalemate with neither side able to inflict a mortal blow to the other. However, the equation changed in 1971 when Pakistan suffered a decisive defeat. Presently Pakistan has a one-to-two disadvantage in land and air forces, and one-to-three on the sea. Although there is approximate parity in the types and quality of weapons systems on both sides, this is also likely to go against Pakistan in years to come. Indian military superiority is unavoidable.

A second element in the nuclear belief is more psychological. Over the years, Pakistanis have developed a collective feeling of gloom and pessimism about the future of the country as they see the continuous deterioration of governance and the inability of the state to deliver on its promises. Key institutions of society are floundering and some have collapsed—these, in fact, were the reasons cited by President Farooq Leghari in dismissing the government of Benazir Bhutto in November 1996. Wholesale corruption has devastated the banking sector and financial institutions. While education and health care of reasonable quality are still available to the tiny minority who can pay for it, public educational and health institutions are barely functional. The population of 130 million has less than 40 million who are literate, newspaper circulation is less than one for 70 persons, clean drinking water is unavailable to the majority of the populace, and on the Human Development Index (HDI) Pakistan ranks 139 out of 175 countries.[5] Sectarian bloodshed and fundamentalist violence in many parts of the country, including ethnic violence in Karachi, have claimed thousands of lives over the last five years. The police and other law-enforcing agencies have been directly involved in large-scale judicial killings, and citizens place little confidence in the ability of the state to administer justice. According to a survey of business practices carried out by Transparency International, Pakistan ranks as the second most corrupt country in the world.[6] No elected government in Pakistan has succeeded in completing its term; the last three governments were removed on grounds of misgovernance and corruption.

Growing institutional malfunction and a feeling of collective failure have understandably led to a steadily deepening crisis for the Pakistani nation. Pride and confidence follow from real achievement; conversely absence of achievement inexorably leads to diminished self-esteem. "Why celebrate Pakistan's fiftieth anniversary? We should mourn, not celebrate," gloomily observed the interim prime minister of Pakistan, Malik Meraj Khalid, at various occasions.[7] More and more Pakistanis in the English language press ask what was gained from partition, although this question still cannot be asked in the conservative Urdu press. The psychological anguish must somehow be made bearable. Enter the bomb.

Kahuta has helped create a sense of achievement in an otherwise bleak environment, and many Pakistanis take mental refuge within its four walls. No longer just a secret laboratory, it has become a sacred symbol which must be protected at all costs. The atomic weapons which are said to be produced there are glittering objects which symbolize mastery of the most sophisticated technology. A country which can manufacture them has presumably proved its mettle. With Kahuta, Pakistan is safe. It cannot be pushed around, called backward, or sent to the bottom of the pecking order of nations.

It is important to understand the extraordinary sense of desperation felt by most Pakistanis as they reel before the rapacity of political and economic elites, and see concern for the common good evaporate. Citizens have become cynical and increasingly disappointed at their historical fate, resulting in a collective loss of confidence in the state. The bomb provides to the masses a refuge from reality and an antidote to collective depression.

The third element underlying the preeminence of the bomb is military dominance of Pakistani decision making. There is a never-ending demand by all militaries for larger and more powerful weapons. Pakistan's military is not unusual in this respect. What is unusual, however, is that it wields absolute power in determining the country's nuclear policy, a matter considered too sensitive to be left for politicians or civilians of any kind to meddle with. It has long been assumed that any government that compromised the nuclear program would be booted out instantly. Both Nawaz Sharif and Benazir Bhutto apparently understand this and have never gone beyond routine assertions of support for the preexisting nuclear policy. Nor have they been reluctant to occasionally play to the gallery with hawkish outbursts. To be fair, however, there is no indication that either disagreed at any level or wished to assert their influence in the nuclear sphere. But were they adequately informed, or did they even seriously wished to be informed, of nuclear details? In Pakistan civilian governments up to the present time have been quite satisfied that nuclear matters are left for the armed forces to decide.[8]

As long as the army controls and gives priority to the nuclear program, Pakistan will continue to develop its nuclear arsenal. The intensity of this commitment, however, will depend on the government in power. Under a possible Islamic government of the future, it will grow rapidly—the rise of the Taliban movement in Afghanistan indicates that this is no idle speculation. Such a government would seek to break the impasse in Kashmir by sending military support across the border more openly, and hence want a still stronger nuclear shield in order to deter an Indian response. There would then be strident calls for an overt declaration of Pakistan's nuclear deterrent and a test explosion.

Nuclear Economics

Next to nothing is known about how much Pakistan spends, or has spent, on its nuclear weapons program. No expenditure figures have ever been released for Kahuta, which houses thousands of high-speed centrifuges for uranium separation and employs about 3,000 workers. Nor are the costs available for the other reported enrichment facility at Golra, the mining and uranium hexafluoride production facilities in Dera Ghazi Khan, or the reactor being built at Khushab for purposes of plutonium production. Also unknown is the cost of weapons development work carried out by the Pakistan Atomic Energy Commission at various secret locations. Unlike India, which is able to hide a good fraction of its weapons development costs within its large civilian nuclear program, Pakistan must pay a premium because it has not integrated nuclear weapons development into its nuclear power program. Yet these costs are completely hidden. No expenditure heading in the government budget reveals weapons-related activities. The budgets are said to be sanctioned by the government and operated directly by the army, probably with few audit checks. The last point is suggested by the abundance of glaring abuses and some very rich bomb makers.

Rumor has it that a total of $4 to $6 billion has been spent over a period of twenty years upon the Pakistani nuclear weapons program.[9] This could be just a shot in the dark, but may not be wholly off the mark; it has been estimated that the Iraqi nuclear program, which achieved much less, consumed between $10 and $12 billion. Accepting, for the sake of argument, the $4 billion figure, the question is: what has been the impact of this spending upon the national economy? One can further ask whether this amount can be doubled, quadrupled, and so forth. What are the limits of this spending?

These questions must be examined in the context of Pakistan's economic profile and overall defense spending, as put forth in the Economic Survey of Pakistan documents periodically issued by the Ministry of Finance. The pie chart below shows that the bulk of government spending in 1994–95, which amounted to 17.7 percent of the total gross domestic product (GDP), was split between debt servicing and defense spending. The servicing of debts, both internal and external, is expected to keep rising in years to come. Defense expenditure as a percentage of GDP increased from 3.2 percent in 1949–50 to 6 percent in 1994–95. Unofficial estimates put defense expenditure as a percentage of GDP at 7 percent for 1996–97 and 7.09 percent for 1997–98.[10] In dollar terms, the GDP in 1994–1995 was about $44 billion, 6 percent of which is $2.64 billion. Divided among 130 million Pakistanis, this amounts to $20 per capita or roughly Rs 840 per Pakistani man, woman, and child.

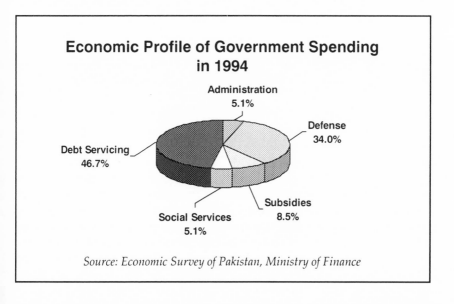

Economic Profile of Government Spending in 1994

Administration 5.1%

Defense 34.0%

Debt Servicing 46.7%

Subsidies 8.5%

Social Services 5.1%

Source: Economic Survey of Pakistan, Ministry of Finance

In spite of its preeminent size, defense spending is a simple one-line entry; only the total amount is stated by the Ministry of Finance. Reasons of national security are supposedly responsible for this blackout on expenditures. What is most interesting, however, is that a retired general of the Pakistan army has recently published some revealing figures:[11]

- From a total of Rs 1.12 billion in 1976, the defense budget has risen to Rs 130 billion in 1996–97, an increase of 115 times over a period of twenty years.
- Between 50 and 60 percent of the army budget is consumed in pay and allowances, and expenditure on pensions will jump from Rs 11 billion in 1996 to Rs 14 billion in 1997, an increase of 27 percent in just one year!

To offset the decrease in purchasing power because of the continuing depreciation of the Pakistani rupee against the U.S. dollar, which amounted to a staggering 30 percent in 1997, the armed forces are expected to demand an enhancement in rupee allocations.

A Pakistani economist, Shahid Kardar, has pointed out that many defense-related items do not feature in the published defense expenditure.[12] For example, the figures do not include debt-servicing costs of officially unacknowledged military debts, or pensions given to defense personnel. In Pakistan as in other countries with high levels of military spending, a substantial portion of the national debt results from the costs of past wars and increases in defense expenditure that were not compensated by an equivalent rise in national revenue. No estimates are available of the share of Pakistan's national debt that is attributable to these military sources, but a comparison with similar figures in the United States may be instructive. According to the Center for Defense Information in Washington, D.C., approximately 39 percent of the U.S. national debt results from past wars and military expenditures.[13] If the military proportion of national debt were equivalent in Pakistan, an additional $1.37 billion would have to be added to the actual cost of military preparedness (39 percent of the annual $3.52 billion debt-service payments). Even if the Pakistani percentage were only half that of the United States, an additional $686 million would be added to the defense burden.

Also not included in the official military budget are allocations made for the various secret services (Rs 4 billion), Civil Armed Forces (Rs 2.7 billion), Pakistan Rangers (Rs 1.8 billion), Frontier Constabulary (Rs 0.7 billion), Ministry of Defense (Rs 1.5 billion), and the Coast Guards (Rs 0.1 billion). The terms of payment on which defense equipment and machinery for defense industries are purchased from foreign suppliers is unknown, the argument being that national security would otherwise be compromised if these were revealed. One can therefore say with some certainty that the declared defense expenditures are less than the actual ones, but there is no hard proof of how much less. However, the exact details are irrelevant to the thrust of the argument which follows.

The key point is that over the years the increase in both debt servicing and military spending has meant that a mere 5 percent of the total budget is left over for all social, economic, and community services. It is clear that the Pakistani state, at the present time, is spending close to every penny that it possibly can on defense. Further squeezing of social programs or cutting back on subsidies and administrative expenditures may yet yield another few percent increase for the armed forces, but the result might be severe social disruption and immense difficulties for whichever government is in power. Those who speak of "making every sacrifice" for the defense of the country must know that, unless Pakistan defaults on its debt payments and is willing to pay the cost of near-total international sanctions, there are very clear and definite limits beyond which it cannot increase its military outlay.

In examining the relative cost of the nuclear weapons program, the earlier estimate of roughly $4 billion over twenty years must be accepted as authentic for lack of a better figure. Broken down, this amounts to an annual $200 million per year. While large, it is not prohibitive when viewed on the scale of major weapons systems. For example, the total cost of the nuclear program is roughly equivalent to that of acquiring forty Mirage 2000-5 fighter aircraft, each having a price tag of some $90 million, for which Pakistan has been negotiating with France ever since the United States withheld transfer of the F-16s paid for by Pakistan. Former chief of army staff General Aslam Beg argues that when Pakistan's nuclear program "was at its peak in 1985, 1986, and 1987, the entire budget of the Kahuta program was less than the cost of one F-16."[14] Two hundred million dollars per year is certainly less than the cost of one French submarine, worth over $300 million, of which Pakistan purchased three in 1995.

While such arguments for nuclear weapons as being "cheap" are seductively persuasive, there is a catch. I do not wish to dwell on arguments of the type that $200 million per year could be used to build x schools and y hospitals and feed z million children. This is a perfectly valid argument, but belongs to a separate domain. Instead, let us accept the assumption that it is relatively inexpensive to acquire a few crude nuclear weapons. This does not, however, constitute a credible or effective nuclear force. To move beyond this stage and acquire a substantial nuclear arsenal of efficient, reliable, and deliverable bombs, together with an adequate command and control system, would be extremely expensive. The cost of nuclear warheads was just 8 percent of the total amount spent by the U.S. on its defense forces since World War II. The superpower experience shows how fast it is possible to go down the steep slippery slope of nuclear escalation.[15] From the day that the first fission bomb was tested in 1945 by the United States, a new dynamic was unleashed. In rapid succession there followed the jet bomber, boosted bomb, fusion bomb, nuclear artillery, intercontinental ballistic missile (ICBM), submarine launched ballistic missile (SLBM), supersonic bomber, multiple independently targeted re-entry vehicle (MIRV) warheads, and so on. Each new development, almost invariably pioneered by the U.S., was followed a few years later by the Soviets until, in 1991, the Soviet Union collapsed from sheer exhaustion.

Some will argue that nuclear racing is not inevitable. If Pakistan has even a handful of bombs, it may be enough to deter an Indian attack. Perhaps. According to General Beg, "Pakistan has acquired the minimum deterrent level . . . . Despite having a massive strength in conventional arms, India cannot dare attack Pakistan because of the fear of a nuclear strike which will render a vast portion of (its) conventional army ineffective."[16] The present state of nuclear ambiguity has held nuclear racing in check, and has thus been to Pakistan's advantage. But should India declare itself an overt nuclear power or conduct a second nuclear test, Pakistan will follow willy-nilly. The Kroc Institute poll shows that 85 percent of those elites who endorse official policy would support weaponization in the event of a second Indian nuclear test. There would then be terrific pressure to deal with enemy countermeasures, upgrade means of delivery, develop sophisticated surveillance systems, and create a workable nuclear command and control system. Whereas initially there may be a fair chance of penetrating enemy defenses, in later stages the nuclear arsenal will have to be greatly enlarged and made more sophisticated to compensate for corresponding increases on the other side. Survivability of the nuclear weapons force would have to be seriously considered since a decapitating strike will certainly be a possibility. Therefore, what may start out as "minimal" is likely to become anything but that with the passage of time.

How would Pakistan finance such a nuclear expansion? There is virtually no elasticity left in the economy. It is, in fact, certain that debt servicing will consume a still larger share of the budget in the years ahead and, therefore, that it will be increasingly difficult for Pakistan to maintain its present level of defense spending, much less increase it. Putting even the last penny into the military is unlikely to make much of a difference. If Pakistan does go all out for a nuclear arms race, the consequent closure of vital social institutions will result in Soviet-style collapse and disintegration. Will India follow the U.S. by instigating its adversary into recklessly overspending on defense and gently maneuver it into collapse? Will Pakistan be able to see the trap before it is too late?

Skill Starvation

Five decades of high defense spending have sharply reduced Pakistan's ability to defend itself by draining away resources from a reservoir which is the source of strength of every modern country—its educational system and a pool of highly skilled people. Today, the abysmal quality of scientific and technical education in Pakistan, and hence the generally poor quality of scientists and engineers employed in national technical institutions, place fundamental limitations on Pakistan's efforts to develop a high-technology-based defense. The indications are that higher education, particularly in the sciences, is in a fast downward spiral, auguring ill both for peaceful and nonpeaceful uses of technology. My contention is that this constraint of poor manpower development will be the essential bottleneck in the development of the country's nuclear program.

The first atomic bomb was an exceedingly brilliant, if terrible, achievement by the world's finest physicists. It required the creation of wholly new physical concepts, based on a then very newly acquired understanding of the atomic nucleus. The ensuing technological effort, the Manhattan Project, was quite unparalleled in the history of mankind for its complexity and difficulty. Today, however, the design and manufacture of atomic weapons is vastly more simple than it was. Basic information is freely available in technical libraries throughout the world. The mysteries of half a century ago are no longer mysteries. The theory of chain-reacting systems, data on critical masses, equations for neutron transport, the assembly-disassembly phase of an exploding device, and so on, are all published. Also available are technical treatments of compression, achievement of "criticality," initiation of chain reactions, buildup of kinetic energy, and the final phases of the explosion as the pieces start to move apart. Advanced textbooks and monographs contain a staggering amount of detail which can enable reasonably competent scientists and engineers to come up with "quick and dirty" designs for nuclear explosives. Benefiting from various declassified documents in the U.S., the general reader as well as the nuclear weapons specialist can now see cut-away drawings of weapons, photographs, and even once-classified test data. The Iraqis, it is now known, made direct use of the Manhattan Project data in their program.

Despite the availability of information, substantial amounts of resources, scientific competence, and engineering ingenuity are still required to make even a crude fission device actually work. It takes intelligence to get complex machines to work and to convert formulas given in books and documents into bomb design parameters. On the other hand, to make advanced weapons—miniaturized bombs, high-yield "boosted" weapons using tritium, and fusion bombs—demands much more in the way of knowledge, skills, and sophistication. To develop these weapons, along with guidance and propulsion systems for missiles and smart weapons, electronic measures and countermeasures, etc., requires a highly integrated military industrial complex staffed by many hundreds of able and competent scientists, backed up by thousands of high-quality engineers and technical support personnel. Will Pakistan be able to achieve this even if it has the material resources? Will it be able to muster the necessary manpower to go beyond the present stage, which it claims to have successfully reached, of making a first generation fission device?

The answer is most probably not, unless there is substantial external assistance from, for example, China. Pakistan's economy is severely skill-starved. This is evident, for example, from the composition of Pakistani labor in the Middle East. The workforce there has increasingly shifted toward the unskilled and semiskilled; the high-paying skilled jobs have long been taken over by Indians, Filipinos, Malaysians, and others. Industries in Pakistan find it difficult to locate skilled professionals, and the lack of a well-disciplined and skilled labor force is the principal reason why the multinationals choose other countries in Asia over Pakistan for manufacturing. Skill starvation is evident in every sector but is particularly glaring in such fields as the operation and maintenance of industrial and domestic electronic equipment, computer repair and programming, industrial process and quality control, operation and maintenance of medical and laboratory equipment and a host of other areas.

Alarmed by the catastrophic state of scientific and engineering education, and realizing that the public sector universities are unsalvageable, the Pakistani establishment is now seeking solutions in a different direction. The Pakistan Institute of Applied and Engineering Sciences, operated by the Pakistan Atomic Energy Commission, is a modern engineering school. So is the National University of Science and Technology, operated by the Pakistani army. The Ghulam Ishaq Institute of Technology is another state-assisted private undergraduate institution. While the quality of these institutions is relatively better, the students studying at these three institutions number only a few hundred.

Pakistan's weakness in technological infrastructure and manpower development has no short-term solutions. To make substantial progress toward developing advanced weapons systems, or to build second- or third-generation nuclear weapons, will be very difficult. Pakistan's failure to develop the Khalid tank and, more significantly, to successfully match India's *Prithvi* missile with an indigenously developed missile, the *Hatf*, are principally due to lack of technical and scientific expertise. Gazing into the crystal ball, it appears that Pakistan will, in years to come, rely ever more heavily upon importation of high-tech items for its defense. However, this requirement will be constrained by the previously mentioned financial limitations. The combination of technical and economic weaknesses may prove insurmountable in curtailing the ambitions of military and nuclear planners.

What Could Limit the Nuclear Race?

Relations between Pakistan and India have oscillated between bad and terrible over the last five decades. Since 1990 these have mostly belonged to the "terrible" category. India has deployed hundreds of thousands of troops to suppress a rebellion in Kashmir that Pakistan actively supports. Many Pakistanis believe that India backs terrorist attacks and bomb explosions in Karachi, Lahore, and other Pakistani cities. In 1994 the two countries claimed that the other's diplomatic mission was a center for terror and subversion. Subsequently, in a tit-for-tat move, the Pakistan consulate in Bombay and the Indian consulate in Karachi were ordered to be closed down and associated diplomats expelled to their respective countries. Although Prime Ministers Gujral and Nawaz Sharif restarted high-level dialogue in 1997, no concrete results have yet emerged from these talks. Relations between the two countries are still marked by occasional serious border disputes, spurts of heated rhetoric, diplomatic incidents, and continued low-level but bloody conflict in Kashmir.

In such a climate of tension and fear, many Pakistanis feel that attempting to negotiate nuclear arms control agreements is futile and should be abandoned. If true, then the future of the subcontinent is very bleak indeed, as the two antagonists wrestle one another, straining to get at each other's jugular. Does this mean that the ordinary Pakistani and Indian citizen, and the world community at large, should then calmly await the nuclear Armageddon because there is nothing to be done? With more than a billion lives at stake, this is a wholly unacceptable and defeatist position. But at the same time, given the level of Indian-Pakistani hostility, one needs to shed illusions that dramatic steps are feasible. In these circumstances the only way to proceed may be through cautious steps which do not call for significant changes in the India-Pakistan nuclear equation, but which nevertheless have important implications for future arms control developments. This may be as far as either country is willing to go at present, but it could still be extremely significant.

Let us briefly survey the types of arms control arrangements that have been proposed and see which, if any, has the potential of being a means toward reducing nuclear tensions on the subcontinent.

The NPT

The Nuclear Nonproliferation Treaty freezes the present division between the five nuclear weapons states and the remaining nonnuclear states, a position that India has rhetorically rejected as "nuclear apartheid." New

Delhi's criticism of the discriminatory nature of the NPT is valid, but the treaty is not without impact. It imposes some limitations on the transfer of weapons-related nuclear technology and reinforces the global norm against nuclear proliferation. India and Pakistan pay a price in diplomatic and political isolation for standing outside the NPT regime. The Kroc Institute poll shows that, although no Pakistani elites favored signing the NPT unilaterally, 95 percent of supporters of official policy and 91 percent of nuclear advocates would be willing to sign the treaty bilaterally with India. The similar Kroc Institute poll conducted in India in 1994 found that 39 percent of educated elites in India would be willing to accede to the treaty if Pakistan were to do so as well.[17] Pakistan has said it will sign the NPT if India does, but neither government has been willing to break with its rhetoric of rejection. For the foreseeable future, the NPT is a lost cause, so far as the subcontinent goes.

South Asian Nuclear Weapon-free Zone

Proposed by Pakistan to the UN General Assembly, this has been repeatedly endorsed by the world community. The most recent vote was on 12 December 1994 when all but 3 nations (India, Bhutan, Mauritius) out of 157 voted in favor. The Indian position is that nuclear weapon-free zones are "illusory" and that it is better to work for a nuclear-free world. New Delhi has consistently refused to consider a bilateral or regional solution to the subcontinent's nuclear standoff, citing the supposed nuclear threat from China. The chances of a nuclear weapon-free zone are zero.

Fissile Materials Cutoff

The excess of fissile materials in the possession of the United States has motivated it to strive for a ban on the production of these materials worldwide, and on the subcontinent in particular. Regardless of this motivation, it would be mutually beneficial for India and Pakistan to agree to cease fissile materials production. India has rejected a regional cutoff, however, again insisting on a global approach and also demanding that civilian stockpiles be exempted. The source of India's weapons-grade plutonium is the reprocessing of waste from its civilian power reactors. An exemption on such materials would make it impossible to have a meaningful treaty.

Pakistan, under pressure from the United States, promised in 1991 not to enrich uranium at Kahuta beyond the 5 percent of U235 limit but refused to allow on-site verification. The quantity of feedstock and the amount of highly enriched uranium is not known. In principle Pakistan agrees with the concept of a fissile materials cutoff but insists that existing stockpiles must be taken into account and that on-site verification not be mandatory. The technical difficulty of verifying the former, and the necessity of including the latter for a meaningful treaty, means that Pakistan's support for a fissile materials cutoff treaty would not automatically follow even if India signed such a deal. In summary, while there seems to be some small amount of room for negotiation, from the subcontinental perspective a fissile materials cutoff treaty also appears to be unattainable.

Comprehensive Test Ban Treaty

The year 1996 saw much bloodletting on the subject of banning nuclear weapons tests. With their nuclear arsenals well-secured, the five nuclear weapons states strongly favored the CTBT as a nonproliferation measure. India, which had supported a test ban as far back as 1952, suddenly found much fault with the CTBT and became a holdout country. During the protracted and painful negotiations of that year, India raised numerous technical objections and, most importantly, insisted that the test ban be linked to a time-bound framework for global nuclear disarmament, a position that drew wide condemnation as a treaty killer. India ultimately voted against the CTBT during the September 1996 General Assembly, again finding itself diplomatically isolated (joined in its rejection by only Bhutan and Libya).

Pakistan, by following a simple reactive policy of declaring that it would not sign the CTBT unless India did, failed to take a step which would have brought it considerable diplomatic and political gain while costing little in military or strategic terms. The "entry into force" clause in the draft treaty specifies that the treaty would not come into effect unless all countries with nuclear programs, including India, Israel, and Pakistan, become signatories. Since Pakistan has no intention of performing a nuclear test—such a step would have extremely serious political and economic consequences—it could easily have signed the treaty unilaterally, knowing that it would not be bound by it until India signed too. However, given that political parties and governments in Pakistan, past and present, are held hostage by the right wing, which would derive immense political capital from propagandizing a unilateral action, Islamabad was unable to act in its own self-interest. Moreover, even the symbolic act of signing the CTBT would be seen by the military establishment as a potential threat since it could legitimize the internal standing of Pakistan's small minority of nuclear opponents, who have, so far, been dismissed as antistate elements for opposing the nuclear "option."

A far more important reason why Pakistani policymakers decided against signing the CTBT despite the pull-out and entry-into-force clauses was the real constraint which this would have imposed on the nuclear program. According to the Vienna Convention of International Treaties, a signatory to a treaty must abide by its provisions even if the treaty has yet to be ratified or has not yet come into force. Withdrawing from an international treaty, moreover, is not a simple procedure and can have adverse diplomatic consequences. If Pakistan had signed the treaty it would have been obligated to forego a possible future nuclear test, an option which the country's military leaders were not prepared to accept.

No Attack On Nuclear Facilities

Pakistan and India agreed in December 1985 to enter into an agreement not to attack each other's nuclear installations. This is the first, and so far only, nuclear agreement between the two. It entered into force on 1 January 1992, and lists of nuclear installations have been exchanged every year since then. Both countries have occasionally accused each other of cheating in the lists, but the agreement has survived. This is heartening, for it shows that there is a recognition, even if partial, of the importance of nuclear negotiations and treaties.

No First Use

A treaty between Pakistan and India to the effect that neither country will initiate the use of nuclear weapons against each other would be an important confidence-building measure. No formal negotiations have been carried out, but it is generally believed that India is for this measure while Pakistan is against it. Pakistan's reasoning, following NATO doctrine in relation to the former Warsaw Pact countries, is that the threat of nuclear weapons use is needed to protect its territory against invasion by a larger adversary. The implication is that, if necessary, Pakistan will use nuclear weapons even if it is attacked by conventional arms.

Should this issue be brought formally to the negotiating table and a positive agreement reached, Pakistan would stand to gain considerably. It makes no sense at all for it to use nuclear weapons under any conditions; while a couple of Indian cities may be severely damaged, the Indian response would leave every single Pakistani city in ruins. Hence, to suggest that nuclear weapons can defend Pakistan is dangerous folly. On the contrary, Pakistan's agreement to no first use could lead to a substantial decrease in nuclear tensions and would force India toward bilateral nuclear discussions, which it has so far spurned.

Tritium Treaty

A tritium agreement would require that India and Pakistan agree not to produce tritium, or attempt to procure it from any source, for military purposes. While this may not be a panacea for Indo-Pakistani nuclear hostility, it may amount to a good beginning and should therefore be vigorously promoted as a possible subject for talks between Pakistan and India.[18] So far this proposal has received no official attention. It deserves a careful hearing, however, for the reasons stated below.

If the first stage of a nuclear race is the development of fission weapons, the second stage involves a new and more destructive type of bomb—the boosted fission weapon using a gas, tritium. This allows the construction of smaller and lighter nuclear weapons that fit in a wider variety of delivery systems. Since neither India nor Pakistan are known to be seriously pursuing the design of boosted weapons, a tritium agreement would have few immediate implications for their respective nuclear programs. Moreover, the design of boosted weapons is far more complex than for ordinary ones and actual physical testing is, in contrast to ordinary atomic bombs, an absolute necessity. In view of the present international environment, however, neither country can dare to explode a test device. Therefore, in realistic terms, boosted weapons are not really a viable option for future development.

What, one might ask, would be gained from an Indo-Pakistani treaty that does not attempt to change nuclear realities, and which seems so inconsequential as to appear almost irrelevant? The answer is, plenty! First, it would be a breakthrough in a situation where there is simply no communication between India and Pakistan on nuclear matters, a highly dangerous state of affairs. Second, the agreement could act as a hurdle that stops, or at least greatly slows down or postpones, the nuclear march toward boosted weapons and the inevitable upward spiral. Third, any type of nuclear agreement would be important as a confidence-building measure and would serve to make possible more meaningful future treaties when political tensions ease.

There are excellent reasons why Pakistan should, and could, support a tritium treaty. First, as the weaker party, it is in Pakistan's interest to contain the subcontinental arms race as best as it can. Second, it is much harder for Pakistan to develop second-generation weapons than for India, and for it to produce tritium in adequate quantities. Third, by engaging India in bilateral talks on the nuclear issue it would score diplomatic points internationally. So far India has refused to talk to Pakistan on nuclear arms elimination or participate in any form of bilateral nuclear negotiations. Finally, the government can enter into such a treaty with India without arousing a great deal of domestic flak from the opposition. The present Pakistan nuclear capability would remain unaffected, and the treaty would be too technical a matter to excite ordinary people.

There are almost equally good reasons for India to want such a treaty. First, it really does not need second-generation weapons to deal with Pakistan and could save much effort and resources by forgoing this option. Although the Chinese card can always be played, the fact is that India's nuclear program is largely aimed at Pakistan. As the first Kroc Institute poll showed, the major security concern of Indian elites is the potential nuclear threat from Pakistan, not China.[19] India already has enough plutonium for at least seventy to eighty Hiroshima bombs, which is more than enough to totally devastate Pakistan. Second, like Pakistan, India would very much like to gain international goodwill, especially if the cost is not high. As a political move a tritium agreement could help soften India's image as an inveterate proliferator which vigorously resisted the CTBT.

To conclude, nuclear war may not be just around the corner—although there is no certainty of that—but poverty and deprivation affect the lives of hundreds of millions of people on the subcontinent. Ever-present is the chance of the ultimate calamity. Drastic remedies, beginning with the measures of the sort discussed in this article, are needed. Will Indians and Pakistanis realize that nuclear weapons do not solve political problems but are a problem in themselves? That they do not make nations great and powerful, or even secure? That the greatest threat to both countries is not from each other but from the social tensions and economic deprivations within each? To bring about this realization and expeditious social change is the fundamental task for peace activists on both sides.

Notes

1. Lt. Gen. Asad Durrani in *Pakistan's Security and The Nuclear Option* (Islamabad: Institute of Policy Studies, 1995), 92.

2. According to the report of the Gandhi Peace Foundation (New Delhi) of 16 January 1996, "Out of 45,000 persons killed in security operations so far, about 40,000 were innocent. About 80,000 are in custody. 18,000 women have been raped. In one village we found 72 boys made impotent. Gandhi's soul must be badly troubled by this brutality."

3. *Fact Sheet on Kashmir*, Institute of Regional Studies, Islamabad, 21 August 1997; *Dawn* (Islamabad), 2 September 1997.

4. Gautum Navlakha, Rita Machandra, and Tapan K. Bose, "Political Situation in Kashmir: Duped by Media and Government," *Economic and Political Weekly*, 20 July 1996, 1927.

5. United Nations Development Programme, *Human Development Report 1997* (New York: Oxford University Press, 1997).

6. President of Transparency International in an interview broadcast on CNN television, 12 December 1996.

7. *The News* (Islamabad), 6 January 1997.

8. There is an interesting question to be asked here: does even the army really know that it has a workable, reliable nuclear weapon? Given that it has no techni-

cal expertise in this area, it must rely upon what it believes to be "expert" opinion. Since the general level of technical personnel is low, one can only assume that it has selected advisors with genuine expertise and competence.

9. It is estimated that $200 million per year has been spent on the Pakistani nuclear program. Alhtar Ali, *Pakistan's Nuclear Dilemma: Energy and Security Dimensions* (Karachi: Economic Research Unit, 1984), 70.

10. Aslam Sheikh, "Arms and People in South Asia," *The News* (Islamabad), 13 April 1997.

11. Lt. Gen. (ret.) Kamal Matinuddin, in *The News* (Islamabad) 13 December 1996.

12. Shahid Kardar in "Defense Spending—How Much is Enough?" (unpublished).

13. Center for Defense Information, *1997 Military Almanac* (Washington, D.C.: Center for Defense Information, 1996), 23; Interview, David Cortright with David Johnson, October 1997.

14. General (ret.) Aslam Beg, "Who Will Press the Button?" *The News* (Islamabad), 23 April 1994.

15. See, for example, a study by Stephen Schwartz on the cost of the U.S. nuclear program, which places the total cost from 1940 to 1995 at a staggering 3.9 trillion dollars. Stephen Schwartz, *The U.S. Nuclear Weapons Cost Study Project* (Washington, D.C.: Brookings Institution, 1997).

16. Beg's comments came at a public seminar in Karachi on 2 April 1994. Ghulam Hussain, "'We Can Have the Bomb within 15 Days in an Eventuality,' says Beg," *Dawn* (Islamabad), 3 April 1994.

17. David Cortright and Amitabh Mattoo, eds., *India and the Bomb: Public Opinion and Nuclear Options* (Notre Dame, Ind.: University of Notre Dame Press, 1996), 39.

18. This proposal was made by Pervez Hoodbhoy in: "Inching towards India-Pakistan Nuclear Peace via a Tritium Agreement," *INESAP Information Bulletin* No. 7 (October 1995); and, "Can Tritium Lead Towards India-Pakistan Nuclear Peace?" *Dawn* (Islamabad), 5 November 1995. A more detailed account, which considers verification issues as well, is contained in Pervez Hoodbhoy and Martin Kalinowski, "The Tritium Solution," *The Bulletin of the Atomic Scientists*, August 1996.

19. Cortright and Mattoo, *India and the Bomb*, 12.

5

Going Nuclear: The Weaponization Option

By Samina Ahmed and David Cortright

This chapter examines the weaponization option for Pakistan. The basic assumption is that Islamabad has the potential to "go nuclear," to weaponize its nuclear program, and that while the choice might be dependent on developments in India, the decision would be made independently. Taking a hypothetical Pakistani determination to go for the weaponization option as the point of departure, the chapter focuses on the security, political, economic, and environmental consequences of such a decision.

With the renewed emphasis on nuclear nonproliferation at the end of the cold war, India and Pakistan have attracted growing international concern. Having fought three wars and been on the brink of armed conflict on several other occasions, India and Pakistan are now de facto nuclear weapons states. This was dramatically illustrated when India decided to test nuclear weapons in May 1998 and Pakistan followed suit soon thereafter. While Pakistan has lagged behind its larger neighbor in the development of nuclear capability, it clearly has the capacity to develop nuclear weapons and could decide to deploy such weapons and integrate them into its armed forces.[1] The consequences of pursuing such a policy are the subject of this chapter.

Historical Context of Pakistan's Nuclear Program

Pakistan's nuclear program, unlike that of India, initially lacked a dominant scientific leader like Homi Bhabha. It was not until I.H. Usmani took over from Nazir Ahmed as chief nuclear scientist and Zulfiqar Ali Bhutto assumed the country's presidency that an effective collaboration between the scientific community and government leaders began to take shape. Pakistan found its Bhabha in Dr. Abdul Qadeer Khan only after India conducted its "peaceful nuclear explosion" in 1974. Although Bhutto advocated a military nuclear program earlier and convened a meeting of nuclear scientists in Multan for this purpose in 1972, the Indian test in 1974 provided the decisive political patronage needed to move the program forward.

Bhutto urged consideration of a military nuclear program while minister for Fuel, Power, and Natural Resources in the 1960s, but then president Ayub Khan focused the nuclear program on civilian energy production. Ayub Kahn's preference for peaceful nuclear energy was partly a result of his confidence in the United States as a strategic ally. He was the main architect of Pakistan's entry into U.S.-sponsored alliances, the South East Asia Treaty Organization (SEATO) and the Central Treaty Organization (CENTO), and he believed that in the case of war between Pakistan and India, Washington would guarantee Islamabad's security. When pressed by Bhutto on developing a military component for the nuclear program, Ayub Khan replied that if a nuclear capability were needed, Pakistan could buy it "off the shelf," apparently referring to the American nuclear program.[2] Bhutto did not share Ayub Khan's confidence in American assistance nor his apparent faith in the peaceful nature of the Indian nuclear program.

Several events motivated the transformation of Pakistan's nuclear program from an exclusively peaceful effort to one with a substantial military component. First was the falling-out politically between Ayub Khan and Bhutto in the wake of the 1965 war and subsequent Tashkent agreement. Ayub Khan's political fortunes ebbed, while Bhutto emerged as a political force in his own right. The dismemberment of Pakistan in the 1971 war also played a major role. As one analyst observed, "Given the ability of Indian armed forces to 'free' any of the remaining constituent territories of Pakistan at will, and the continuing difficulty of the Indo-Pakistan leadership to evolve a peaceful, coexistent *modus vivendi,* it was hard for the Pakistani elite as well as the public to feel confident about the future integrity and security of their country."[3] The Indian nuclear test in 1974 provided additional momentum and proved decisive in creating support for a more active military nuclear program. President Bhutto pressed ahead with the weapons program. Dr. A. Q. Khan was placed in charge of a new nuclear organization separate from the Pakistan Atomic Energy Commission (PAEC) and given the mandate to develop the capacity for enriching uranium to weapons-grade quality. An ambitious undertaking was also mounted to recruit Pakistani students and scientists living abroad to participate in the nuclear program.

Subsequent Pakistani governments have continued the steady development of the nuclear weapons program. President Zia ul-Haq ironically benefited from the Soviet invasion of Afghanistan, which prompted Washington to turn a blind eye to the nuclear program and to provide the F-16 aircraft that could be used as a potential nuclear weapons delivery system. When the United States reimposed nonproliferation sanctions in the wake of the Soviet withdrawal from Afghanistan, Pakistan offered the minor concession of capping its uranium enrichment program but otherwise maintained the momentum of its nuclear development program. By the early 1990s Pakistan had acquired nuclear weapons capability, as confirmed by the declaration of Foreign Secretary Shaharyar Khan during a trip to Washington in 1992. Then former prime minister Nawaz Sharif flatly declared in August 1994 that Pakistan possessed nuclear weapons. These assertions were tempered, however, by Dr. A.Q. Khan, who told newsmen in 1995 that "some politicians . . . get carried away in the heat of the moment to declare that Pakistan already possesses the bomb." He went on to say that "Pakistan has acquired a nuclear capability and if and when a decision is made, producing the bomb will only be an academic question." He made it clear that the policy of not producing actual weapons was "a political decision and Pakistan has stuck to it."[4] These statements read together show a deliberate attempt at creating ambiguity regarding Pakistan's nuclear program.

Pakistan's position has remained consistent over the years despite changing political alignments and international conditions. The official line continues to be that Pakistan has the capability to weaponize its nuclear program but that it will do so only if India weaponizes its program or detonates another nuclear explosion. Islamabad's approach to arms control diplomacy also remains fixed. Pakistan says it will sign the Nuclear Nonproliferation Treaty, NPT, only if India signs. Islamabad has proposed a number of regional solutions to the nuclear quagmire in South Asia, but India consistently rejects these suggestions, arguing that denuclearization must be international, encompassing China and all the nuclear weapons states. The result is a continuing diplomatic impasse.

The Motivations for Weaponization

There is broad consensus in Pakistan on maintaining the nuclear option, but support for weaponization is more limited. The Kroc Institute survey found 61 percent of all respondents supporting the present policy of nuclear ambiguity, but only 32 percent in favor of actually developing nuclear weapons. However, the survey also found that under certain scenarios, support for weaponization would increase. When supporters of official policy were asked what could justify Pakistan developing nuclear weapons, 85 percent identified another Indian nuclear test. The other development that would most significantly motivate respondents to support weaponization would be Indian deployment of the *Prithvi* and/or *Agni* missiles (72 percent of official policy supporters). These findings indicate deep-seated concern about India's development of weapons of mass destruction. Respondents also expressed concern about the prospect of a further conventional arms advantage for India. Among supporters of official policy, 36 percent identified a further conventional advantage as possible justification for the development of nuclear weapons. None of the other factors identified in the survey—a worsening of relations with other nations, turmoil within the country, or increased international pressures—were considered a justification for weaponization.

The Indocentric basis of support for nuclear weapons development is evident from responses to other questions in the survey as well. One hundred percent of nuclear advocates cited "threats from India" as the reason for developing nuclear weapons. Forty-eight percent of all respondents expressed approval for a Pakistani nuclear test. But this figure jumped to 73 percent under the scenario of India conducting a second nuclear test. When asked about the extent of Pakistani nuclear weapons development, 96 percent expressed support for developing a nuclear arsenal capable of striking only India. These results confirm the singularity of the threat from India as the dominant justification for nuclear weaponization in Pakistan.

Military Capabilities and Security Consequences

The size and extent of a Pakistani nuclear arsenal, should the government decide to develop one, can only be estimated. No official reports on the subject are available. The best estimates come from Western researchers, who believe that Pakistan has developed sufficient weapons-grade material to produce approximately fifteen nuclear weapons. Pakistan may also have the capacity to produce additional weapons on an annual basis if it were to commit to full-scale weaponization. A reasonable estimate, therefore, is that Pakistan might have as many as twenty-five quickly deployable nuclear weapons with a capacity to produce a limited number of additional weapons annually.

Pakistan's systems for delivering nuclear weapons are limited but sufficient for the small number of weapons available. The air force provides the primary delivery capability through fifty-six French-supplied Mirage 5s and thirty-four U.S.-produced F-16s.[5] Although not originally configured for nuclear weapons delivery, these planes could be adapted to that purpose. Pakistan is developing an indigenous ballistic missile production program, but the capability of these systems remains uncertain. The short- and medium-range *Hatf I* and *Hatf II* missiles, with ranges of 80 and 300 kilometers respectively, have been tested but their accuracy is problematic. China has reportedly transferred M-11 ballistic missile technology to Pakistan, but both Islamabad and Beijing deny these allegations. U.S. intelligence sources quoted by American analysts report that Pakistan may possess 30 nuclear-capable M-11 missiles with a 280 to 300 km range.[6] In April 1998 Pakistan tested the new *Ghauri* medium-range ballistic missile with a reported range of 1,500 kilometers. The reliability of these systems and their capacity to deliver nuclear weapons remain uncertain.

The limited capabilities noted above offer Pakistan few military options for the actual use of nuclear weapons. Pakistani delivery systems do not have the ability to penetrate deeply into Indian territory. Pakistan is only capable of targeting the western and northwestern parts of India. This could put New Delhi and Bombay in jeopardy, along with Pokhran and several other nuclear production sites. But much of India would remain out of range, and India would retain an overwhelming retaliatory capacity. Limitations in the accuracy and reliability of Pakistan's delivery systems make the prospect of a first strike or precision attack extremely remote. Moreover, while there is no proof that Pakistan has the capability of mating nuclear weapons to the missiles supplied by China, lack of strategic depth also makes Pakistan's airbases vulnerable to attack, thereby putting the survivability of its main delivery system at risk.

The only possible use for Pakistan's nuclear weapons would be to raise dramatically the cost for India should it attempt a nuclear or conventional military attack. The presumed scenario for the Pakistani military would be to launch desperation strikes against high-value targets such as Bombay in the event of an Indian attack. Anything beyond this most basic deterrent function would seem to be beyond Pakistani military and nuclear capabilities.

Nuclear hawks in Pakistan (and India) extol the utility of weaponization and overt deterrence by pointing to the example of the U.S.-Soviet cold war. The nuclear standoff between the superpowers supposedly prevented world war and gave an element of predictability to their relationship. Similar benefits might result in South Asia, nuclear proponents argue. Overt weaponization would stabilize the region, reduce tensions, and avert the danger of war. It would also have the additional advantage for Pakistan, advocates assert, of eliminating the need for reliance on unpredictable external support. The chief proponent of the nuclear hard-line in Pakistan is General K.M. Arif, retired vice chief of army staff, who has stated, "Let India and Pakistan both become nuclear weapons states openly and without reservations. They are both mature nations which need no counseling on their international responsibilities and conduct."[7] Claiming that nuclear weapons have prevented war in South Asia, Arif states, "nuclear weapons have helped to maintain peace in Europe. During the four-decade-long cold war, the fear of mutual self-destruction prevented their use. A similar scenario can be obtained elsewhere."[8]

The attempt to superimpose the U.S.-Soviet cold war model on India and Pakistan is fundamentally flawed and fraught with danger. As Pervez Hoodhboy has noted,

> In the U.S.-USSR deterrence system, a massive system of early warning systems, both space- and ground-based, was needed to detect missile launchers. In spite of a relatively long flight time of 20 to 25 minutes, the systems remained severely strained and are authoritatively known to have generated false messages of attack. The existence of redundant and multiple safeguards prevented accidental war, but the margin was not comfortable.[9]

In the case of India and Pakistan, early warning systems are practically nonexistent. The borders are contiguous rather than separated by thousands of miles, and the maximum flight time is five to seven minutes. The margin for error is razor thin, and any mistake or miscalculation could lead to catastrophe.

Command and Control

Nuclear hawks assume that, once a commitment to overt weaponization is made, the command and control systems required for effective nuclear strategy will be produced as well. The assumption is highly questionable, however, since neither country, especially Pakistan, has the necessary human and technological resources to develop the elaborate and redundant command and control systems required for the use of these deadly weapons.

Credible information about nuclear command and control systems in Pakistan is not available.[10] The assumption is that this capability, like the nuclear program as a whole, is tightly under the command of the armed forces. Several major obstacles confront the development of an effective command and control system. The most fundamental is geostrategic. The flight times of missiles are so short and the strategic depth of Pakistan so narrow that commanders lack sufficient time to evaluate and act upon warning of attack. The likely response in such circumstances would be launch on warning or immediate strategic retaliation. Reliable warning information would be crucial, but absolute assurances of accuracy are simply not possible given the rudimentary state of Pakistani intelligence capabilities. The intelligence arm of the armed forces, Inter-Services Intelligence (ISI), lacks access to military spy satellites.[11] Its capacity for remote intelligence gathering is unknown but likely to be limited. The combination of immediate decision-making requirements and primitive intelligence gathering is unstable and potentially dangerous.

Effective control of nuclear weapons requires a degree of transparency and predictability in the military operations and political relations of the countries involved. Each side must have confidence in the command system of the other. Political leaders must be able to contact each other during periods of crisis and verify whether warnings of attack are true or false. But nuclear ambiguity and the predominance of military control in Pakistan undermine these requirements. If political leaders continue the charade of neither confirming nor denying nuclear capability, decision makers will not know whether, for example, a flight of approaching F-16s or Mig fighters is armed with conventional or nuclear weapons. An Indian prime minister calling his counterpart in Pakistan has the additional problem of not knowing if the Pakistani leader is actually in control of nuclear decision making. For all of the dangers involved in the U.S.-Soviet nuclear competition during the cold war, there was at least a degree of predictability and openness about the nuclear policies of the two countries, and nuclear weapons on each side were under tight civilian political control. The uncertainty about these factors in South Asia adds another element of instability to the current nuclear equation.

An additional concern is the possibility of accidental or inadvertent launch. This is a special problem in Pakistan, where nuclear weapons are under the exclusive control of the armed forces, with little or no role for elected leaders. Safety measures to guard against inadvertent use are standard equipment in the United States and the other nuclear weapons states. Permissive action links (PALS) block arming mechanisms unless proper authorization codes are entered. The standard "two-man" rule requires positive action by two individuals to activate launch systems. It is unknown if these systems exist within the Pakistani armed forces. It seems highly unlikely that Pakistan has been able to acquire PALS technology from the United States, given the nonproliferation restrictions in U.S. law. Lacking access to advanced control technologies, and commanded by a military hierarchy with little or no civilian oversight, the Pakistani nuclear program would appear to be highly vulnerable to the risk of inadvertent use. This vulnerability, combined with the limitations mentioned earlier, compounds the dangers inherent in the Pakistani nuclear program.

Concern about an inadvertent war between India and Pakistan which escalates into a nuclear exchange has been frequently voiced by U.S. intelligence and policy-making circles. Testifying before the Senate Intelligence Committee, for example, CIA director George Tenent stated that, "Although neither side wants war, the two sides could stumble into it, most likely as a result of misperceptions of each other's intentions or military postures." Assistant Secretary of State for Intelligence and Research Toby Gati warned that "the Kashmir dispute remains a possible flashpoint for regional war, with the potential to escalate into a nuclear exchange" between two geo-

graphically contiguous, "mutually suspicious states, each seemingly convinced that nuclear weapons are an essential attribute of major power
status."[12]

An example of how inadvertent war could take place between Pakistan and India is illustrated by the Ojheri incident of 10 April 1988, when
an explosion took place at the Ojheri ammunition depot situated in a
heavily populated area in the twin cities of Rawalpindi and Islamabad.
Rawalpindi is the general headquarters of the Pakistani military, and
Islamabad the federal capital; not far away is Kahuta, Pakistan's main
uranium processing facility. The April 1988 explosion in the supply depot
used for stockpiling weaponry for the Afghan resistance caused extensive
destruction and hundreds of casualties and sent heat-seeking missiles,
rockets, and projectiles into population centers in both cities. The damage
included a temporary breakdown of telecommunications in the federal
capital and at military headquarters, resulting in widespread rumors of
an Indian attack on the Kahuta facility.[13]

Had the Kahuta plant been hit by one of the missiles, the release of
radioactivity would have caused enormous human and environmental
damage.[14] Even more serious consequences could have resulted from the
incident. The debate on the disaster in the National Assembly and disclo-
sures by top military commanders, including the commander of the 10th
Corps at Rawalpindi, established that the existence of the depot was known
only to military dictator General Zia ul-Haq and Inter-Services Intelligence,
which controlled the clandestine operation of supplying arms to the Afghan resistance.[15] The combination of the three factors—the proximity of
military headquarters, the federal capital, and the Kahuta nuclear facility;
the breakdown in communications; and a weak command and control
structure—could have created a chain of misperception and miscalculation leading to accidental or inadvertent war. Since both Pakistan and India were nuclear capable by 1988, such a conflict could have included a
nuclear dimension.

In any scenario, inadvertent or intentional, in which a decision is taken
by Pakistan to use nuclear weapons, the lack of effective command and
control over nuclear weapons and the limited extent of its nuclear capabilities mean that Pakistan will be forced to rely on only the most rudimentary form of military doctrine. Elaborate options for limited strikes or
gradual escalation are simply impossible. The only option available for
the use of nuclear weapons would be to launch a desperate strike in the
face of overwhelming attack, but such a strike could only reach part of
India and would leave it capable of retaliating with devastating power.
The likely result of a Pakistani strike would thus be immediate Indian
retaliation and the resulting total devastation of Pakistan. The presumed
security benefits of nuclear capability turn out to be an illusion. Far from

protecting Pakistan from its giant neighbor, nuclear weapons capability would place the nation in even greater jeopardy.

External Pressures

Apart from its impact on the security environment in South Asia, a decision to develop and deploy nuclear weapons would have substantial negative impacts on Pakistan's relations with the broader international community. Of particular concern is the negative reaction of the United States. Under the Nuclear Proliferation Prevention Act passed by the U.S. Congress in 1994, Washington is required to terminate all assistance and financial loans to any nonnuclear state, including Pakistan or India, that conducts a nuclear test or engages in overt nuclear weapons activity. The act also prohibits private U.S. banks from providing credit, and thus reduces financing for important development projects. The act contains no waiver provisions. When India detonated five nuclear devices in May 1998, the White House immediately imposed the required sanctions. When Pakistan followed suit, the same sanctions were imposed on it. As a result, Pakistan has been cut off from important sources of U.S. financial support. The economic consequences could be severe. Capital investment may dry up, and inflation and unemployment could increase. The resulting hardships for the public and private sectors could increase poverty and social suffering. Military cooperation programs and arms deliveries have also come to a standstill.

In India, with its large and diverse economy and high rates of growth in recent years, the impact of U.S. sanctions is likely to be limited. In Pakistan, however, the results will be serious. The economy of Pakistan is weaker than India's and more susceptible to disruption. Pakistan has been experiencing a balance of payments crisis and is heavily dependent on IMF funding to meet debt obligations and maintain basic services. Currency reserves are dangerously low. In such a condition, Pakistan is highly vulnerable to U.S. sanctions.

Pressures against Pakistan would come not only from the United States but from European countries and Japan as well. In the past the United States has convinced France and other governments to cooperate in nonproliferation sanctions against Pakistan (the most famous case being Paris's cancellation of a contracted nuclear reprocessing plant in the 1970s). Similar or even greater pressures would develop in the event of a decision by Islamabad to weaponize its nuclear capability. According to the former chairman of the Pakistan Atomic Energy Commission, Munir Ahmed Khan, France reluctantly rescinded the nuclear reprocessing plant agreement in the 1970s because it "could not afford to take on the U.S. which was in a position to make things difficult for France in other areas such as commercial, military, and political."[16] Munir Ahmed Khan has opposed overt weaponization, warning that such a course would place Pakistan's economic and technological cooperation with "major donors and collaborators under strain. This is particularly true in the case of Japan, which is the largest donor of aid to Pakistan, and Germany which attaches high priority to nonproliferation."[17]

A cutoff of investment and assistance from Japan, Pakistan's major trading partner, would be particularly disastrous. While Japan does not always follow the U.S. lead in international diplomacy, and often is hesitant to impose sanctions, it is possible that on an issue of this importance, the proliferation of nuclear weapons capability in Asia, Japan would join international efforts to pressure Islamabad. In fact, Japan has consistently pressured Pakistan to reverse its nuclear weapons policy, attempting to use incentives, such as aid, to gain influence with Pakistani policymakers. During the visit of the Japanese foreign minister to Islamabad in July 1997, for example, Japan granted Pakistan $17.8 million in aid, but Yukihiko Ikeda pressed Pakistan to sign the CTBT, expressing Japan's "deep concern" about nuclear proliferation in South Asia.[18]

Pakistan's ability to withstand such pressures would depend greatly on the reaction of China, an increasingly important strategic partner for Islamabad. While China signed the NPT and has endorsed the general international norm against nuclear proliferation, it has provided active support for Pakistan's military and nuclear programs. News reports based on U.S. intelligence agency sources indicate that Beijing has supplied nuclear materials, reactor and enrichment technology, ballistic missiles, and other military equipment.[19] China has also been reluctant to support sanctions against potential proliferators. During the 1993–94 crisis over North Korea's nuclear program, China blocked efforts within the UN Security Council to consider the imposition of sanctions against Pyongyang. Beijing undoubtedly would be similarly reluctant to support sanctions against Islamabad. China's strategic interest in supporting Pakistan as a counterweight to India and its increasingly close ties with the Pakistani military would probably override pressures from other countries to join in efforts to isolate Islamabad.

Pakistani leaders view their partnership with China as the country's ace in the hole, its guarantee against international isolation and hostility. But how reliable and supportive a partner would China be if Pakistan were to weaponize its nuclear capability and become an international pariah? Beijing's interest in cooperation with Islamabad is limited. Beijing benefits from a partnership that helps to keep New Delhi off balance and preoccupied with regional concerns and that solidifies its credentials with the Islamic world. But it would not favor extremist policies in Islamabad and wishes to avoid the outbreak of full-scale warfare in Kashmir. A worsening of Indo-Pakistani relations and an overt nuclear arms race in the subcontinent would not be in China's interests. It is unlikely that China would jeopardize its larger international interests to support Pakistan on a course of greater nuclear confrontation. In October 1997, as Jiang Zemin prepared to visit the United States, some observers in Islamabad feared that China would agree to end its nuclear cooperation with Pakistan in exchange for the lifting of the U.S. ban on nuclear reactors and technology.[20] Pakistani generals were relieved when the nuclear agreement between China and the United States covered Iran rather than Pakistan, but they could not have been reassured at Beijing's willingness to bargain for its own advantage at the expense of an erstwhile partner. The prospect of a similar fate for Pakistan in the future cannot be ruled out, especially if Islamabad were to embark on a more adventurous course. Pakistan's partnership with China would not compensate for the greater hostility and isolation that would result from a decision to go nuclear. Diminished financial assistance from the major powers and declining diplomatic support internationally would be unavoidable.

On the other hand, it is possible that international pressures against Pakistan might produce a "rally around the flag" effect domestically and strengthen political resolve within the country. Pakistani nationalists point to past U.S. sanctions—the Glenn-Symington amendment and the Pressler amendment—and assert that if Pakistan was able to withstand such pressures in the past it will survive even greater pressures in the future. Such evocations of patriotic fervor make for good politics, but they underestimate the severity of the economic damage resulting from the sanctions regime initiated by the United States. Past sanctions efforts have been inconsistent and poorly implemented and have never been comprehensive in nature. The kinds of economic pressures imposed following the decision to test nuclear weapons are tougher and more wide ranging. This has not prevented Pakistani leaders from exhibiting their nationalist credentials and declaring that they will not bend to Western demands. The results of the Kroc Institute survey confirm widespread public support for a posture that rejects the pressure of sanctions. When respondents were asked if a threat of international sanctions would justify the renunciation of nuclear weapons, not a single person responded affirmatively. When supporters of official policy were asked if nuclear weapons could be renounced in exchange for incentives such as preferential trade agreements and access to economic aid and advanced technology, only 2 percent responded positively.

A deeply rooted sense of national pride and a long and bitter experience with on-again off-again sanctions from the United States have reinforced a fierce sense of independence among Pakistanis. Moreover, on the vital and emotive issue of Kashmir, Pakistan has long been without friends and allies. This was driven home recently when Islamabad found itself alone in tabling a resolution against Indian atrocities in Kashmir before the UN Human Rights Commission. Neither the United States nor China have been willing to give diplomatic or political support to Pakistan's position on the Kashmir issue. Because Pakistan has so little international support on this crucial issue, many political leaders believe they have nothing to lose from further international isolation. Hard-liners in Pakistan argue that the country's interests in Kashmir will not be jeopardized by the international political fallout resulting from the decision to test nuclear weapons. Some even argue that weaponization is the "stick" that Pakistan might use to gain the "carrot" from the West of greater involvement in and support for its position on Kashmir. This is a very high stakes and risky gambit, however, that could backfire and deepen the country's isolation. The flag of Pakistani patriotism has become tattered over the decades by corruption, ethnic strife, and other political ills, and attempts to rally around it are likely to be ineffective over the long term. The economic and political costs of international isolation could soon overwhelm the initial enthusiasm of rallying to the national cause.

Domestic Dynamics

The argument is sometimes made that nuclear weapons can enhance a nation's legitimacy and forge greater unity within the society. Nuclear weapons for Pakistan, according to Rodney Jones, "would strengthen the unity of the country and, in that sense, its security."[21] While nuclear weapons capability might give a greater sense of strength and legitimacy to military and political leaders, the benefit for the rest of society would be questionable. The public might initially rally around a national crusade for nuclear weapons, but the ability to sustain that support, as noted above, would probably erode as costs and negative consequences mounted. Indeed the social consequences of overt weaponization for the majority of Pakistanis could be disastrous. The harsh international reaction to Pakistan's decision to test nuclear weapons will generate severe pressures on the nation's economy and society. The consequences of the U.S. embargo will create enormous strain on the government and its allocation of resources among competing social groups and interests. The sharp cleavages that already exist within Pakistani society, which have led to communal violence in Sindh and Punjab, will probably be exacerbated by the economic and social hardships generated by external coercion. The resulting increase in social tensions, including the prospect of greater communal violence, may further weaken civilian political authority and give greater justification to continued military dominance of government and society.

The political impact of nuclear weaponization within Pakistan is likely to be a further entrenchment of the armed forces as a dominant force in political decision making. Pakistan is already a heavily militarized society, of course, where generals have ruled openly in the past and remain the power behind the throne today, setting the context and limiting the parameters within which civilian authorities can rule. The very fact that Prime Minister Benazir Bhutto was not informed about the country's nuclear weapons development program, despite being the country's senior elected leader, vividly illustrates the limitations of civilian rule, especially in vital matters of national security.

When the nuclear program first began it was argued that the development of nuclear weapons would strengthen civilian control over the armed forces. This was a justification that Zulfiqar Ali Bhutto employed in his advocacy for the nuclear option. Bhutto asserted that because of the supreme political importance for the nation of the potential use of nuclear weapons, control over such issues must inevitably rest with civilian political authorities, not the armed forces. The assumption was that the generals would never arrogate to themselves the decision to develop and possibly use nuclear weapons, and that the very existence of the nuclear program would provide a means by which civilian authorities could gain greater control over defense strategy and doctrine. Obviously Bhutto's vision was not realized, as evidenced by his daughter's inability to know about much less control the status of nuclear weapons in Pakistan. Nonetheless, it is at least conceivable that the existence of an overt nuclear weapons capability might prompt civilian political authorities to exert greater control over the program, and by implication over defense planning generally.[22] While such a development is theoretically possible, the history of the nuclear program to date, and of civil-military relations in general, provides ample grounds for skepticism. It is just as likely that overt weaponization would lead to a further consolidation of military control.

Proponents of nuclear weaponization sometimes contend that nuclear weapons are "cheaper" than conventional ones, providing "more bang for the buck." Some assume that a nuclearized national defense policy might even allow for military budget savings. This is an illusion. If anything, a nuclear arsenal would add additional resource requirements and financial burdens. Mirage and F-16 planes would have to be adapted to nuclear roles, security forces trained and deployed, and expanded nuclear production facilities developed. Command and control systems would have to be substantially upgraded. Additional delivery systems such as M-11 missiles from China would also have to be acquired. Depending on the scale of the weaponization option, these additional costs would double or triple the estimated $200 million spent annually on the nuclear program.[23] The overall level of military spending would rise, not fall.

A nuclear weapons capability would not replace the need for conventional forces. The security threat justifying Pakistan's large armed forces, the threat posed by its giant neighbor to the east, would not diminish with the weaponization of the nuclear option. In fact it would probably increase as India adopted countermeasures in response to Pakistan's actions. According to a staunch opponent of overt weaponization, former PAEC chairman Munir Ahmed Khan, India would be "the major gainer" if Pakistan decided to opt for weaponization. A Pakistani test would, for example, provide India "the perfect justification for overt resumption of its nuclear weapons program. In response to our fission device, India may test a fusion device. . . . A new round of nuclear escalation will begin, taxing our resources" and the "stakes will get higher and higher."[24] Under these circumstances Pakistan would not reduce but increase its conventional armed forces. Weaponization of the nuclear option would add new economic burdens on top of those already imposed by Pakistan's huge military budget.

Little or nothing is known about the health and safety implications of Pakistan's nuclear program. With the public and even the prime minister kept in the dark about the details of the program, it is not surprising that information about environmental consequences is virtually nonexistent. Nonetheless, public anxiety about potential environmental costs is high. One of the surprising findings of the Kroc Institute survey was the high degree of concern about environmental impacts evident among all respondents. Ninety-two percent of those interviewed agreed with the statement that "a civilian nuclear energy program has high environmental costs attached." Even among nuclear advocates, 88 percent agreed with this assertion. Seventy percent of all respondents agreed that "the costs of a civilian nuclear energy program far outweigh its benefits." While these statements referred to the civilian nuclear program rather than the military effort, it is unlikely that respondents would consider the military program any safer than its civilian counterpart. Overt weaponization, entailing a larger nuclear production program, would probably increase these concerns. Additional reactors, enrichment facilities, and reprocessing plants would be necessary for an expanded program, which would multiply the risks of environmental contamination. Concerns about the health consequences of nuclear production surfaced recently at the uranium mining and processing center in Dera Ghazi Khan, as reported by Zia Mian in chapter 3. These concerns would undoubtedly grow with a larger and more active nuclear production program.

Engaging Civil Society

The depth of public concern about environmental hazards illustrates the potential for public opinion to act as a constraint on Pakistani nuclear policy. This is especially important in relation to the weaponization option. A decision to pursue overt nuclear development would be a major departure from current policy and would require political leaders to win public backing and perhaps overcome domestic opposition. The Kroc Institute poll found only 32 percent of those interviewed in support of weaponization, with 61 percent favoring the official policy of ambiguity. The poll also found some skepticism about the nuclear option in general. As noted in chapter 1, while only 6 percent of all respondents favored complete nuclear renunciation, 16 percent of those supporting official policy agreed that "under no circumstances" would Pakistan be justified in developing nuclear weapons. These indications of potential opposition exist despite the steady drumbeat of official rhetoric in favor of the nuclear option and the strident tone of many public statements about India. That so many people remain opposed to or skeptical of further nuclear development suggests that obtaining public support for the costs and risks associated with overt nuclear weaponization could be difficult.

If public opinion is to serve as a constraint on nuclear policy more generally, civil society in Pakistan will need nurturing and support. Some groups of Pakistani citizens have joined hands with their Indian counterparts to promote peace between their two countries and to oppose the nuclear and conventional arms race. The Association of Peoples in Asia, in its Indo-Pak Amity meeting of May 1996 in New Delhi, called for a "reduction in arms purchases and stoppage of the nuclear arms race in this continent."[25] The India-Pakistan People's Forum for Peace and Democracy has urged both states to start direct talks to eliminate the danger of nuclear conflict, passing a resolution in Lahore in 1995 that urged India and Pakistan to "immediately initiate direct dialogue aimed at reducing and eventually eliminating the chances of a nuclear war by intent or accident, irrespective of any international negotiations or agreements."[26] Citizen initiatives such as these are limited, however. Support for denuclearization does not extend much beyond a very small segment of Pakistan's educated elite. Since information about nuclear weapons policy is almost impossible to obtain and government propaganda dominates the broadcast and print media, few Pakistani citizens are able to form a truly informed opinion.

With the nuclear enterprise hidden from public scrutiny and the discourse on security policy dominated by the armed forces, the prospects for educating and arousing public opinion are bleak. Overcoming these obstacles will require the strengthening of democracy through respect for human rights, increased literacy and transparency, and greater political accountability. Most importantly, the development of civil society will require a reduction in the power of the armed forces and the elevation of civilian authority and institutions. These are essential steps for democratizing Pakistan and advancing the prospects for denuclearization. The United States and other major powers have an important role to play in this process. External support is crucial to the government in Islamabad. With 45 percent of the national budget devoted to debt servicing and the armed forces heavily dependent on foreign sources of supply and technology, Pakistan is potentially vulnerable to pressures or inducements from abroad. Decisions made in Washington, Beijing, Tokyo, and other capitals can have an enormous impact in Islamabad and can shape the options available to Pakistani leaders. As noted in chapter 1, Washington has recently embarked on a new policy of engagement with Pakistan and India, although this approach has been complicated by the recent imposition of sanctions under the Proliferation Prevention Act. In general, incentives policies have many benefits, but they can also generate unintended negative consequences. Much depends on what is being offered and to whom it is being delivered. Incentives policies should be sensitive to the internal political dynamics of the recipient country and should seek to empower those forces which are most likely to adopt reform policies. Incentives delivered to military forces or to corrupt and repressive elites can undermine the standing of constituencies supporting democratic reform and weaken the prospects for reform. Targeting incentives to empower the supporters rather than the opponents of reform is crucial to the effective design and implementation of inducement policies.

Unfortunately, U.S. incentives policies to date have channeled benefits primarily to the armed forces rather than civil society. The Brown amendment's package of military equipment and the Harkin-Warner amendment's proposed resumption of military training benefited the armed forces and thereby provided support for those who have trampled democracy and championed the nuclear option. No conditions or requirements were attached to these offers of aid, signaling Washington's apparent abandonment of efforts to encourage nuclear restraint. Not only were no conditions attached to these offers of assistance, but they came despite repeated Pakistani declarations of nuclear capability and assertions that its weapons program is nonnegotiable. The most recent of these gestures of defiance came from Nawaz Sharif in August 1997 just prior to his meeting with President Clinton at the UN in New York and only a few weeks after Senate passage of the Harkin-Warner amendment. The prime minister asserted that Pakistan has "a certain nuclear capability" and asked Washington to stop pressuring Pakistan on the nuclear issue, declaring that, "we consider this issue behind us, and the Pakistani nation does not want to discuss it."[27] The Clinton administration ignored the statement and proceeded with the meeting, thereby signaling its implicit acceptance of Nawaz Sharif's terms. Washington's new policy of engagement thus offered diplomatic engagement and military assistance for a Pakistani leadership that continued to develop an expensive and risky nuclear weapons program to the detriment of its own people.

A better approach would be to direct incentives to civil society. Inducements and benefits should be offered to those who have a potential interest or stake in alternative policies. This would mean empowering civilian institutions and social movements that have called for reordered spending priorities, or that have campaigned for human rights and democracy. It means strengthening the rule of law and offering protections for those who dissent from official policy. Institutional support should be provided to groups within the Pakistani parliament and elsewhere which seek to create a more informed public debate on security policy. Many people resent the fact that the Pakistani military budget is presented as a single line item in the national budget, with no subheadings or breakdown of costs and thus no way of knowing what is spent on nuclear weapons. No discussion is allowed on this issue, and indeed no debate is possible when the information upon which it would be based is not available. The U.S. and other external powers could do much to promote democracy by encouraging greater transparency and when necessary by providing direct support to those organizations and groupings which seek to collect and disseminate critical information on military and nuclear policy. Support should also be provided to programs which improve literacy, especially among women, and which seek to encourage greater diversity of opinion in the print and broadcast media.

One of the declared objectives of U.S. policy in Pakistan is the promotion of democracy. Yet American officials have refused to comment upon or take action against systematic human rights abuses and the undermining of democracy. When human rights abuses occur in China, U.S. diplomats are vociferously critical, but when similar abuses occur in Pakistan, American officials are strangely and inappropriately quiet. This silence implies tacit acceptance and belies the stated goal of encouraging democracy. The United States should be consistent in its promotion of democracy, criticizing abuses wherever they occur and providing concrete support to the victims of abuse and to those who struggle for a freer and more open society.

One of the most powerful incentives tools available to the United States and other external powers would be the partial forgiveness of debt. Such an approach was recommended in the 1997 report of an independent task force of the U.S. Council on Foreign Relations, *A New U.S. Policy Toward India and Pakistan*, but no specific plan was offered for how to implement such a policy. As we suggest in chapter 1, bilateral donors and international financial institutions should develop a program of forgiving portions of Pakistan's huge external debt in exchange for specific commitments toward reform. Such a policy could have an enormously beneficial economic and social impact within Pakistan, freeing up vast financial resources for critically needed human development programs. To be effective as a nonproliferation or demilitarization initiative, such a policy should include clear understandings that the money saved from reduced debt service payments must be directed to nonmilitary social development purposes. This would in effect be a "debt for development" swap, loosely modeled on the debt for nature swaps that have been implemented by international financial institutions.

The program could begin slowly, offering forgiveness for limited portions of Pakistan's external indebtedness, but could gradually expand as donor nations and institutions were assured that resources are devoted to nonmilitary purposes. This emphasis on economic development would help to ensure a wide social constituency in support of the debt forgiveness program and would empower constituencies to work for reform and demilitarization as a means of ensuring the continued flow of resources. In this way the proposed debt forgiveness program would aid social development while simultaneously providing resources and support for the empowerment of civil society. This kind of incentives policy would provide genuine political and social benefits. It would encourage the development of a less militarized, more democratic society in which an open and informed debate on the nuclear option could at last take place. Perhaps then the people of Pakistan could more freely assess the full implications of the nuclear program and begin to develop an alternative security policy that pursues peace and cooperation rather than constant military confrontation.

Notes

1. In 1994, former chief of army staff General Mirza Aslam Beg disclosed that Pakistan had acquired nuclear components by 1987 and possessed the knowledge and means to assemble nuclear weapons. Ghulam Hussain, "'We Can Have the Bomb in 15 Days in an Eventuality,' says Beg," *Dawn* (Islamabad), 3 April 1994.

2. President Ayub turned down Bhutto's proposal to purchase an Rs. 300 million reprocessing plant, indicating his disinterest in pursuing a military nuclear program. General (ret.) Mirza Aslam Beg, "Taking Down the Nuclear Fence," *The News* (Islamabad), 2 January 1995.

3. Shirin Tahir-Kheli, *The United States and Pakistan: The Evolution of an Influence Relationship* (New York: Praeger, 1982), 119.

4. "Qadeer on Nuclear Issue," *The Nation* (11 June 1995): 6.

5. *The Military Balance 1996/97* (London: The International Institute for Strategic Studies, 1996), 66.

6. Bill Gertz, "Pakistan Deploys Chinese Missiles," *Washington Times*, 12 June 1996.

7. Quoted in Pervez Hoodbhoy "Overt Better Than Covert? What Declaring the Bomb would Mean," *The News* (Islamabad), March 1993.

8. General (ret.) Khalid Mahmud Arif, "Nuclear Option in South Asia," *Dawn* (Islamabad), 4 February 1994.

9. Hoodbhoy, "Overt Better Than Covert?"

10. S. Hidayat Hasan, "Command and Control of Nuclear Weapons in Pakistan," *Swords and Ploughshares: The Bulletin of the Program in Arms Control, Disarmament, and International Security at the University of Illinois* 9, no. 1 (Fall 1994): 12–13.

11. Ibid., 14.

12. *The News* (Islamabàd), 6 February 1997.

13. Air Marshall (ret.) Ayaz Ahmed Khan, "The Ojheri Depot Explosion," *The Muslim* (Islamabad), 12 April 1988. See also *Dawn* (Islamabad), 11 April 1988.

14. Farhatullah Babar, "Raining Missiles in the Capital: Some Baffling Questions," *The Muslim* (Islamabad), 14 April 1988.

15. *Dawn* (Islamabad), 13 November 1989.

16. Munir Ahmed Khan, "Franco-Pak Nuclear Relations," *The News* (Islamabad), 31 October 1994.

17. Munir Ahmed Khan, "Price of Nuclear Rhetoric," *The News* (Islamabad), 14 September 1994.

18. *Dawn* (Islamabad), 23 July 1997 and 25 July 1997.

19. David Albright, Frans Berkhout, and William Walker, *Plutonium and Highly Enriched Uranium 1996: World Inventories, Capabilities, and Policies* (New York: SIPRI, Oxford University Press, 1997), 166–67. Bill Gertz, "Pakistan Deploys Chinese Missiles," *The Washington Times*, 12 June 1996, 1.

20. *Dawn* (Islamabad), 15 October 1997.

21. Rodney Jones, "Pakistan's Nuclear Options," in *Soviet American Relations with Pakistan, Iran and Afghanistan,* ed. Hafeez Malik (London: MacMillan), 212.

22. Ibid.

23. Akhtar Ali, *Pakistan's Nuclear Dilemma: Energy and Security Dimensions* (Karachi: Economic Research Unit, 1984), 70.

24. Munir Ahmed Khan, "To Test or Not to Test," *The News* (Islamabad), 15 May 1997.

25. *Mainstream*, 17 August 1996, 31.

26. *The Asian Age*, 13 November 1995.

27. *Dawn* (Islamabad), 16 August 1997.

Appendices

Appendix A

Complete Results and Tabular Data of the Kroc Institute Opinion Survey

TABLE 1: Stance on Nuclear Issues
Questions 6 and 25

	All	Arts, Sports, Social	Acad., Sci.	Bur., Dipl.	Bus.	Jour.	Law	Pol.	Med.	Arm. Frc., Pol.	Other
Base (In actual numbers)	910	51	84	201	237	49	80	109	68	28	3
(Figures below are percentages)											
Official Policy Supporters Pakistan should maintain its official position on nuclear issues	61	47	44	72	46	63	78	79	60	68	33
Nuclear Advocates Pakistan should develop nuclear weapons	32	16	20	24	54	27	23	20	40	18	67
Nuclear Opponents Pakistan should renounce nuclear weapons	6	37	36	0	0	10	0	0	0	0	0
No Opinion	1	0	0	0	0	0	0	1	0	0	0

TABLE 2: Rating of Issues
Questions 1 and 2

	All	Supporters of Official Policy	Nuclear Advocates	Nuclear Opponents	No Opinion
Base (in actual numbers)	910	554	290	54	12

(Figures below are percentages)					
Economic stability	53	56	49	46	45
Kashmir	56	58	54	43	55
Ethnic conflict and religious sectarianism	54	56	51	57	35
Afghan refugee presence	43	50	32	36	30
Nuclear weapons issue	28	18	45	52	15
Poverty	48	50	44	51	60
External military assistance and weapons supply	6	5	9	2	10
Political polarization	5	3	7	9	20
IMF/World Bank pressure for economic restructuring	6	5	8	4	30
Percent considering nuclear issue very important	80	83	72	100	75

TABLE 3: Availability of Information on Nuclear Issues
Question 4

	All	Supporters of Official Policy	Nuclear Advocates	Nuclear Opponents	No Opinion
Base (in actual numbers)	910	554	290	54	12
(Figures below are percentages)					
Information on nuclear issues is easily available	1	2	0	7	0
information on nuclear issues is not so easy to get	7	9	0	28	0
Information on nuclear issues is neither easy nor difficult to get	21	22	18	39	8
Information on nuclear issues is difficult to get	50	52	51	17	50
Information on nuclear issues is almost impossible to get	20	15	31	9	42

TABLE 4: Level of Knowledge About Nuclear Policy
Question 3

	All	Supporters of Official Policy	Nuclear Advocates	Nuclear Opponents	No Opinion
Base (in actual numbers)	910	554	290	54	12
(Figures below are percentages)					
Pakistan's nuclear policy is a major area of interest for me professionally	6	6	5	11	0
I am well informed about Pakistan's nuclear policy	24	24	27	15	0
I am informed about Pakistan's nuclear policy just enough	63	67	57	67	25
I have never really paid any attention to Pakistan's nuclear policy	7	4	11	7	75

TABLE 5: Influence on Nuclear Policy
Question 18

	All	Supporters of Official Policy	Nuclear Advocates	Nuclear Opponents
Base (in actual numbers)	898*	554	290	54
(Figures below are percentages)				
I have/had significant influence on Pakistan's nuclear policy	2	1	4	4
I have/had marginal influence on Pakistan's nuclear policy	6	2	10	17
I have/had no influence on Pakistan's nuclear policy	37	34	43	28
I am/was not related in any way to Pakistan's nuclear policy	56	63	43	52

*Total base figure under "All" category for tables 5, 14, 15, and 16 equals 898 instead of 910. This is because those listing "No Opinion" in question 6 are not included in this calculation.

TABLE 6: Opinion about Civilian Nuclear Energy Program
("Strongly Agree" and "Somewhat Agree")
Question 5

	All	Supporters of Official Policy	Nuclear Advocates	Nuclear Opponents	No Opinion
Base (in actual numbers)	910	554	290	54	12
(Figures below are percentages)					
A civilian nuclear energy program can help meet Pakistan's energy deficit	94	94	96	83	100
The benefits of a civilian nuclear energy program far outweigh its costs	23	19	27	35	0
A civilian nuclear energy program can be more harmful than beneficial	12	13	10	15	0
The costs of a civilian nuclear energy program far outweigh its benefits	70	70	72	72	0
A civilian nuclear energy program has high environmental costs attached	92	96	88	94	0

TABLE 7: Could Pakistan Renounce Nuclear Weapons Under Any Circumstance?
Questions 8a and 11a

	Supporters of Official Policy	Nuclear Advocates
Base (in actual numbers)	554	290
(Figures below are percentages)		
A final settlement with India on the Kashmir dispute	71	81
A verifiable renunciation of India's nuclear option	42	87
Nuclear protection from the U.S. and/or China	0	0
A threat of international sanctions	0	0
A global ban on nuclear tests, freeze on the production of nuclear materials, and a time-bound plan for global nuclear disarmament	25	18
If India's conventional arms advantage is reduced	49	69
Preferential trade agreements and access to economic aid and advanced technology	2	0
Diplomatic and political supports to Pakistan's position on Kashmir	11	7
Under no circumstances	3	0

**TABLE 8: Should Pakistan Sign the
Nuclear Nonproliferation Treaty?
Questions 8b and 11b**

	Supporters of Official Policy	Nuclear Advocates
Base (in actual numbers)	554	290
(Figures below are percentages)		
Unilaterally	0	0
Only if India does the same	95	91
Under no circumstances	4	9

TABLE 9: Why Pakistan Should Develop Nuclear Weapons
Question 9

	Nuclear Advocates
Base (in actual numbers)	290
(Figures below are percentages)	
Threats from India	100
Threats from Russia	0
Threats from other nuclear powers	1
Threats of economic sanctions	0
Increased international pressures on Pakistan's domestic policies	0
To improve Pakistan's bargaining power in world affairs	3
To enhance Pakistan's international status	1
To protect and enhance the security of the Islamic world	0

TABLE 10: Should Pakistan Renounce Nuclear Weapons?
(Sign the Nuclear Nonproliferation Treaty?)
Question 12

	Nuclear Opponents
Base (in actual numbers)	54
(Figures below are percentages)	
Unilaterally and sign the NPT	15
Unilaterally and not sign the NPT	9
Bilaterally with India and sign the NPT	76
Bilaterally with India and not sign the NPT	0

TABLE 11: Why Pakistan Should Renounce Nuclear Weapons
Question 13

	Nuclear Opponents
Base (in actual numbers)	54
(Figures below are percentages)	
Nuclear weapons are morally repugnant	39
A nuclear Pakistan would become the target of the major nuclear powers	6
A nuclear war would destroy Pakistan	0
Nuclear weapons do not address the primary threats to Pakistan's security, i.e., ethnic conflict and political polarization	4
Pakistan cannot afford nuclear weapons	17
Nuclear weapons production harms the environment	80

TABLE 12: Could Anything Justify Pakistan Developing Nuclear Weapons?
Questions 7 and 14

	Supporters of Official Policy	Nuclear Opponents
Base (in actual numbers)	554	54
(Figures below are percentages)		
India conducts another nuclear test	85	54
India deploys its *Prithvi* and/or *Agni* missiles	72	20
India gains a further conventional arms advantage	36	22
A serious deterioration in relations with Russia	0	0
A breakdown of Pakistan's relations with Western countries	0	0
Increased turmoil in the country requires a new rallying symbol for national unity	0	0
Threats from other nuclear powers	0	0
Threats of economic sanctions	0	0
Increased international pressure on Pakistan's domestic policies	2	0
Under no circumstances	16	28

TABLE 13: To What Extent Should Pakistan Develop Nuclear Weapons?
Question 10

	Nuclear Advocates
Base (in actual numbers)	290
(Figures below are percentages)	
Develop a nuclear arsenal capable of striking Russia and India	0
Develop a nuclear arsenal capable of striking only India	96
Develop a nuclear arsenal capable of striking all nuclear powers, i.e., Great Britain, U.S., France China, Russia, and India	1
Develop all components but not actually assemble any nuclear weapon	3

TABLE 14: When Could Pakistan Use Nuclear Weapons?
Question 15

	All	Supporters of Official Policy	Nuclear Advocates	Nuclear Opponents
Base (in actual numbers)	898	554	290	54
(Figures below are percentages)				
If India were about to attack Pakistan across the international border	98	99	98	89
If India were to intervene militarily across Kashmir's Line of Control	77	77	81	56
If a major Islamic state were threatened	0	0	0	0
If a U.S.-led coalition of countries were to intervene militarily	0	0	0	0
Accidentally	1	1	2	2
Never	1	1	0	4

**TABLE 15: Extent of Support for International Agreement
Eliminating Nuclear Weapons
Question 16**

	All	Supporters of Official Policy	Nuclear Advocates	Nuclear Opponents
Base (in actual numbers)	898	554	290	54
(Figures below are percentages)				
Totally support	61	71	37	98
Support to some extent	36	27	58	2
Neither support nor oppose	3	2	4	0
Oppose to an extent	0	0	0	0
Totally oppose	0	0	1	0

TABLE 16: When Will an International Treaty be Signed?
Question 17

	All	Supporters of Official Policy	Nuclear Advocates	Nuclear Opponents
Base (in actual numbers)	898	554	290	54
(Figures below are percentages)				
The next five years	52	54	45	76
The next ten years	39	39	44	19
The next twenty years	6	5	7	6
Never	2	2	3	0

TABLE 17: Would You Approve of a Test to Develop Pakistan's Nuclear Capability?
Question 19

	All	Supporters of Official Policy	Nuclear Advocates	Nuclear Opponents	No Opinion
Base (in actual numbers)	910	554	290	54	12
(Figures below are percentages)					
Approve	48	36	73	20	100
Disapprove	52	64	27	80	0

TABLE 18: Should Pakistan Conduct a Nuclear Test If India Conducts a Second Test?
Question 20

	All	Supporters of Official Policy	Nuclear Advocates	Nuclear Opponents	No Opinion
Base (in actual numbers)	910	554	290	54	12
(Figures below are percentages)					
Approve	73	68	93	17	100
Disapprove	27	32	7	83	0

TABLE 19: Demographic Profile
Questions 22, 23, 24a, and 27

	All	Supporters of Official Policy	Nuclear Advocates	Nuclear Opponents	No Opinion
Base (in actual numbers)	910	554	290	54	12
(Figures below are percentages)					
Sex:					
Male	93	94	92	83	92
Female	7	6	8	17	8
Age:					
Up to 39 years	11	10	10	20	42
40 to 49 years	27	25	29	43	33
50 t0 59 years	40	42	38	31	25
Over 60 years	22	23	24	6	0
Education:					
Graduate (Gen.)	32	36	23	37	25
Graduate (Prof.)	17	17	21	13	8
Postgraduate (Gen.)	19	16	24	22	25
Postgraduate (Prof.)	16	13	22	17	33
Doctorate	6	5	8	11	0
Under-graduate, etc.	10	13	4	0	8
Awards received:					
Academic awards	1	1	0	2	0
Military awards	6	6	6	13	0
Civil awards	3	3	4	2	0
None	90	90	90	83	100

TABLE 20: Political Affiliation
Question 21

	All	Supporters of Official Policy	Nuclear Advocates	Nuclear Opponents
Base (in actual numbers)	910	554	290	54
(Figures below are percentages)				
Pakistan People's Party	5	6	4	6
Muslim League (Nawaz) (PML-N)	23	25	18	13
Muslim League (Junejo) (PML-J)	0	0	0	0
PML (Qasmi)	0	0	0	0
PML (Pagara)	0	0	0	0
Awami National Party (ANP)	0	0	0	0
ANP (Haqeeqi)	0	0	0	0
MQM (Altaf)	7	8	7	6
MQM (Haqeeqi)	0	1	0	0
Jamhoori Watan Party (JWP)	1	1	0	2
BNM (Hayee Group)	0	0	0	0
BNM (Mengal)	0	0	0	0
Pakhtunkhawa Mille Awami Party	0	0	0	0
Pakistan National Party (Bizenjo)	1	1	0	2

TABLE 20: Political Affiliation (con't)

	All	Supporters of Official Policy	Nuclear Advocates	Nuclear Opponents
Base (in actual numbers)	910	554	290	54
(Figures below are percentages)				
Jamaat-i-Islami	1	1	2	0
JUI (Fazlur Rehman)	0	0	0	0
JUI (Darkhwasti Group)	0	0	0	0
JUP (Noorani Group)	0	0	0	0
JUP (Niazi Group)	0	0	0	0
Sindh National Front	0	0	0	0
Jiye Sindh (G.M. Syed)	0	0	0	0
Jiye Sindh (Taraqqi Pasand Party)	0	0	0	0
Tehriq-i-Nifaz Fiqah Jafaria	0	0	0	0
Sipah-i-Sahaba Pakistan	0	0	0	0
PPP (Bhutto Group)	0	0	0	0
Tehriq-i-Istaqlal	0	0	0	0
None	62	58	69	72
Other	0	0	0	0

Appendix B
Survey Questions

Q. 1. (See Table 2)

There are various issues which are discussed and considered important by different people. We have some of them listed here. Please take a look at this card and tell us which of these issues/problems facing our country today do you consider to be important, next important, etc.? (Continue until respondent ranked five.)

ISSUE/PROBLEM
Economic stability
Kashmir
Ethnic conflict and religious sectarianism
Afghan refugee presence
Nuclear weapons issue
Poverty
External military assistance and weapons supply
Political polarization
IMF/World Bank pressure for economic restructuring

Q. 2. (See Table 2)

Focusing on the nuclear issue, how important do you personally find it to be? Please respond with the help of this card. (Check one only.)

Very important
Somewhat important
Neither important nor unimportant
Somewhat unimportant
Very unimportant

Q. 3. (See Table 4)

Which of these statements is most true of you? (Check one only.)

Pakistan's nuclear policy is a major area of interest to me
    professionally
I am well informed about Pakistan's nuclear policy
I am informed about nuclear policy but just enough
I have never really paid any attention to Pakistan's nuclear policy

Q. 4. (See Table 3)

Often we might find it difficult to get information on certain issues, while information on others is very readily available and publicized. Talking about the nuclear issue, which of these statements best describes your opinion on availability of information on this issue?

Information on nuclear issues is easily available
Information on nuclear issues is not so easy to get
Information on nuclear issues is neither easy nor difficult to get
Information on nuclear issues is difficult to get
Information on nuclear issues is almost impossible to get

Q. 5. (See Table 6)

Talking about civilian nuclear energy, the people we have met so far have expressed varying opinions about civilian nuclear energy. I will now read out some of the opinions to you. As I read each out, please tell me with the help of this card, to what extent you agree or disagree with each.

Strongly agree
Somewhat agree
Neither agree nor disagree
Somewhat disagree
Strongly disagree

STATEMENT
A civilian nuclear energy program can help meet Pakistan's
    energy deficit
The benefits of a civilian nuclear energy program far outweigh
    the costs

A civilian nuclear energy program can be more harmful
    than beneficial
The costs of a civilian nuclear energy program far outweigh
    its benefits
A civilian nuclear energy program has a high environmental
    cost attached

Q. 6. (See Table 1)

As you must be aware, Pakistan has developed the technical capability
of producing nuclear weapons. Our official position is that we have not
manufactured a nuclear weapon/device despite our ability to do so. While
Pakistan supports global and regional nuclear nonproliferation on a nondiscriminatory basis, we are unwilling to foreclose our nuclear option in
the present circumstances or sign the Nuclear Nonproliferation Treaty
(NPT).

In light of the above, which one of these statements best describes your
feelings on the issue?

STATEMENT	INSTRUCTIONS
Pakistan should maintain its official position on the nuclear issue	Go to Q. 7
Pakistan should develop nuclear weapons	Go to Q. 9
Pakistan should renounce nuclear weapons	Go to Q. 12
No opinion/Don't know/Cannot say (Only if volunteered)	Go to Q. 19

Q.7. (See Table 12)
(Q.7, 8a, and 8b asked only if 1 was selected in Q.6)

You said that you would like Pakistan to renounce its nuclear option
and maintain its official position on the nuclear issue.

However, in your opinion which one or more of these circumstances
could justify Pakistan developing nuclear weapons?

India conducts another nuclear test
India deploys its *Prithvi* and/or *Agni* missiles
India gains a further conventional arms advantage
A serious deterioration of relations with Russia

A breakdown of Pakistan's relations with the Western countries
Increased turmoil in the country which requires a new rallying
    symbol for national unity
Threats from other nuclear powers
Threats of economic sanctions
Increased international pressures on Pakistan's domestic policies
Under no circumstances

Q. 8a. (See Table 7)

Could Pakistan renounce nuclear weapons under one or more of the
following circumstances?

A final settlement with India on the Kashmir dispute
A verifiable renunciation of India's nuclear option
Nuclear protection from the U.S. and/or China
A threat of international sanctions
A time-bound plan for global nuclear disarmament
If India's conventional arms advantage is reduced
Preferential trade agreements and access to economic aid and
    advanced technology
Diplomatic and political support for Pakistan's position
    on Kashmir
Under no circumstances

Q. 8b. (See Table 8)

Even if Pakistan does renounce nuclear weapons, which of these best
describes your opinion on whether Pakistan should sign the NPT?

Pakistan should sign the NPT
    OPTIONS   **INSTRUCTIONS**
    Unilaterally
    Only if India does the same
    Under no circumstances   Go to Q. 15

Q. 9. (See Table 9)
(Q. 9, 10, 11a, and 11b asked only if 2 was selected in Q. 6)

You said that you want Pakistan to develop nuclear weapons. Which
one or more of these are your reasons for saying this?
Threats from India

Threats from Russia
Threats from the other nuclear powers
Threats of economic sanctions
Increased international pressures on Pakistan's domestic policies
To improve Pakistan's bargaining power in world affairs
To enhance Pakistan's international status
To protect and enhance the security of the Islamic world

Q. 10.   (See Table 13)

Even as a nuclear country, Pakistan could take various steps. Some of these are written on this card. Which of these best describes your opinion of what Pakistan should do?

Develop a nuclear arsenal capable of striking Russia and India
Develop a nuclear capability of striking only India
Develop a nuclear arsenal capable of striking all nuclear powers
   i.e., Great Britain, the U.S., France, Israel, China, Russia, and India)
Develop all the components but not actually assemble any nuclear
   weapons

Q. 11a.   (See Table 7)

Could Pakistan renounce nuclear weapons under one or more of the following circumstances?

A final settlement with India on the Kashmir dispute
A verifiable renunciation of India's nuclear option
Nuclear protection from the U.S. and/or China
A threat of international sanctions
A global ban on nuclear tests, freeze on the production of nuclear
   weapons material, and a time-bound plan for global nuclear dis-
   armament
If India's conventional arms advantage is reduced
Preferential trade agreements and access to economic aid and
   advanced technology
Diplomatic and political support to Pakistan's position on Kashmir
Under no circumstances

Q. 11b.   (See Table 8)

Even if Pakistan does renounce nuclear weapons, which of these best describes your opinion on whether Pakistan should sign the NPT?

Pakistan should sign the NPT:
    OPTIONS   **INSTRUCTIONS**
    Unilaterally
    Only if India does the same
    Under no circumstances   Go to Q. 15

Q. 12. **(See Table 10)**
        (Q. 12, 13, and 14 asked only if 3 was selected in Q. 6)

You said you would like Pakistan to renounce nuclear weapons. Which of these statements best describes the conditions on which Pakistan should renounce nuclear weapons?

    Unilaterally and sign the NPT
    Unilaterally and not sign the NPT
    Bilaterally with India and sign the NPT together
    Bilaterally with India and not sign the NPT

Q. 13. **(See Table 11)**

Which one or more of these are your reasons for wanting Pakistan to renounce nuclear weapons?

    Nuclear weapons are morally repugnant
    A nuclear Pakistan would become the target of the major nuclear
        powers
    A nuclear war would destroy Pakistan
    Nuclear weapons do not address the primary threats to Pakistan's
        security, i.e., ethnic conflict and political polarization
    Pakistan cannot afford nuclear weapons
    Nuclear weapons production harms the environment

Q. 14. **(See Table 12)**

However, would you consider Pakistan going nuclear under any of these circumstances?

    India conducts another nuclear test
    India deploys its *Prithvi* and/or *Agni* missiles

India gains a further conventional arms advantage
A serious deterioration of relations with Russia
A breakdown of Pakistan's relations with the Western countries
Increased turmoil in the country which requires a new rallying
symbol for national unity
Threats from other nuclear powers
Threats of economic sanctions
International pressures on Pakistan's domestic politics
Under no circumstances

Q. 15. (See Table 14)
(Q. 15, 16, 17, and 18 asked only if 1, 2, and 3 were selected in Q. 6)

If Pakistan does acquire a nuclear arsenal, under which of these circumstances could the nuclear weapon be used?

If India were about to attack Pakistan across the international
border
If India were to intervene militarily, across the Line of Control in
Kashmir
If a major Islamic state were threatened
If a U.S.-led coalition of countries were to intervene militarily
Accidentally
Never

Q. 16. (See Table 15)

To what extent do you support an international agreement for the elimination of all nuclear weapons?

Totally support
Support to some extent
Neither support nor oppose
Oppose to some extent
Totally oppose

Q. 17. (See Table 16)

Do you think an international treaty banning nuclear weapons could be signed in:

The next five years?

The next ten years?
The next twenty years?
Never?

Q. 18.   (See Table 5)

Which of these statements is most true of you?

I have/had significant influence on Pakistan's nuclear policy
I have/had marginal influence on Pakistan's nuclear policy
I have/had no influence on Pakistan's nuclear policy
I am/was not related in any way to Pakistan's nuclear policy

Q. 19.   (See Table 17)

To develop its nuclear capability, if Pakistan were to explode an atomic bomb, would you approve or disapprove?

Approve
Disapprove

Q. 20.   (See Table 18)

As you may know, India conducted a nuclear test twenty-two years ago at Pokhran. If India were to conduct a second nuclear test today, would you approve or disapprove of Pakistan conducting a nuclear test?

Approve
Disapprove

Q. 21.   (See Table 20)

Which of these political parties, if any, do you support?

Pakistan People's Party (PPP)
Muslim League (Nawaz) (PML-N)
Muslim League (Junejo) (PML-J)
PML (Qasim)
PML (Pagara)
Awami National Party (ANP)
ANP (Haqeeqi)

Mohajir Qaumi Movement (Altaf) (MQM-A)
MQM (Haqeeqi) (MQM-H)
Jamhoori Watan Party (JWP)
Baluchistan National Movement (BNM) (Hayee Group)
BNM (Mengal)
Pakhtunkhawa Mille Awami Party (PKMAP)
Pakistan National Party (Bizenjo)
Jamaat-i-Islami
Jamiat Ulema-i-Islam (Fazlur Rehman)(JUL-F)
JUI-Darkhwasti Group
Jamiat Ulema-i-Pakistan (JUP) (Noorani)
JUP-Niazi
Sindh National Front
Jiye Sindh (G.M. Syed Group)
Jiye Sindh Taraqqi Pasand Party
Tehriq-i-Nifaz Fiqah Jafaria
Sipah-i-Sahaba Pakistan
Pakistan's Peoples Party (Shaheed Bhutto Group)
Tehriq-i-Istaqlal
None
Others (please specify _____)

Q. 22. (See Table 19)

Sex of respondent?
Male
Female

Q. 23. (See Table 19)

Age of respondent?

39 years or younger
40 to 49 years
50 to 59 years
60 years or over

Q. 24a. (See Table 19)

Educational background of respondent

Graduate (General)
Graduate (Professional)
Postgraduate (General)
Postgraduate (Professional)
Doctorate

Q. 24b.

Degree held _____ Subject _____

Q. 25.   (See Table 1)

Respondent's field of work?

Academics	Politics
Science	Business
Bureaucracy	Armed Forces
Diplomacy	Police
Law	Fine Arts
Journalism	Sports
Medicine	Other
Social Work	

Q. 26.

Designation (or level) held currently/at time of retirement

Vice Chancellor
Reader/Professor
School/College Principal
Joint Secretary or above
Member of Parliament
     (National/Provincial Assembly)
Freelance Journalist
Justice—Supreme Court
Justice—High Court
NGO Representative
Practicing Lawyer
Editor/Assistant Editor
Sr. Consultant Doctor

Inspector General (Police)
Deputy Inspector General (Police)
Major General or above
Rear Admiral or above
Air Vice Marshal or above
Director or above (Public sector)
Chairman/MD (private sector)
Others (Please specify)

Q. 27. (See Table 19)

Have you been the recipient of any official Pakistani civil or military awards?

Please specify:

Bibliography

Books

Albright, David, Frans Berkhout, and William Walker. *Plutonium and Highly Enriched Uranium, 1996: World Inventories, Capabilities, and Policies.* New York: SIPRI/Oxford University Press, 1997.

Ali, Akhtar. *Pakistan's Nuclear Dilemma: Energy and Security Dimensions.* Karachi: Economic Research Unit, 1984.

Arif, Khalid Mahmud. *Working With Zia: Pakistan's Power Politics, 1977–1988.* Karachi: Oxford University Press, 1995.

Arnett, Eric, ed. *Military Capacity and the Risk of War: China, India, Pakistan, and Iran.* Oxford: Oxford University Press, 1997.

———. *Nuclear Weapons After the Comprehensive Test Ban: Implications for Modernization and Proliferation.* Stockholm: Stockholm International Peace Research Institute, 1996.

Bajpai, Kanti, and Stephen P. Cohen, eds. *South Asia After the Cold War: International Perspectives.* Boulder, Colo.: Westview Press, 1993.

Bajpai, Kanti et al. *Brasstacks and Beyond: Perception and Management of Crisis in South Asia.* New Delhi: Manohar, 1995.

Beg, Mirza A. Raquib. *Random Thoughts.* Karachi: Mohsin Sayed Jaffri, 1991.

Betts, Richard K. *Nuclear Blackmail and Nuclear Balance.* Washington, D.C.: Brookings Institution, 1987.

Bhutto, Zulfikar Ali. *If I Am Assassinated.* New Delhi: Vikas, 1979.

Bouton, Marshall et al. *Preventing Proliferation in South Asia: The Report of a Study Group.* New York: The Asia Society, 1994.

Burki, Shahid Javed. *Pakistan Under the Military: Eleven Years of Zia ul-Haq.* Boulder, Colo.: Westview Press, 1991.

Center for Defense Information. *1997 Military Almanac.* Washington, D.C.: Center for Defense Information, 1996.

Chari, P.R. *Indo-Pak Nuclear Standoff: The Role of the United States.* New Delhi: Manohar, 1995.

———. *Managing Nuclear Proliferation in South Asia: An Indian View.* College Park, Md.: Project on Rethinking Arms Control, Center for International and Security Studies at the University of Maryland, 1995.

Chari, P.R., Pervaiz Iqbal Cheema, and Iftekharuzzaman, eds. *Nuclear Non-Proliferation in India and Pakistan: South Asian Perspectives.* New Delhi: Monohar, 1996.

Chitkara, M.G. *Nuclear Pakistan.* New Delhi: APH Publishing Corporation, 1996.

Chopra, Pran. *India, Pakistan, and the Kashmir Tangle.* New Delhi: Indus, 1994.

Chow, Brian G. *Civilian Nuclear Programs in India and Pakistan*. Santa Monica, Calif.: RAND, 1996.

Cohen, Stephen P. *The Pakistani Army*. Berkeley: University of California Press, 1984.

———, ed. *Nuclear Proliferation in South Asia: The Prospects for Arms Control*. Boulder, Colo.: Westview Press, 1991.

Contemporary Problems of Pakistan. Boulder, Colo.: Westview Press; Lahore, Pakistan: Distributed by Pak Book, 1993.

Cortright, David and Amitabh Mattoo, eds. *India and the Bomb: Public Opinion and Nuclear Options*. Notre Dame, Ind.: University of Notre Dame Press, 1996.

Finnis, John, Joseph M. Boyle, and Germain Grisez. *Nuclear Deterrence: Morality and Realism*. New York: Oxford University Press, 1987.

Fischer, David. *Stopping the Spread of Nuclear Weapons: The Past and the Prospects*. London: Routledge, 1992.

Fukuyama, Francis. *The Security of Pakistan: A Trip Report*. Santa Monica, Calif.: RAND, 1980.

Fuller, Graham. *Islamic Fundamentalism in Pakistan: Its Character and Prospects*. Santa Monica, Calif.: RAND, 1991.

Gallup. *Pakistani Public Opinion on Nuclear Issues*. Islamabad: Gallup Pakistan, 1996.

Gauher, Altaf. *Ayub Khan: Pakistan's First Military Ruler*. New York: Oxford University Press, 1996.

Gottfried, Kurt, and Bruce G. Blair. *Crisis Stability and Nuclear War*. New York: Oxford University Press, 1988.

Independent Task Force, Council on Foreign Relations. *A New U.S. Policy Toward India and Pakistan*. New York: Council on Foreign Relations, 1997.

Ispahani, Mahnaz. *Pakistan: Dimensions of Insecurity*. London: Brassey's, for the International Institute for Strategic Studies, 1990.

Jalal, Ayesha. *The State of Martial Rule: The Origins of Pakistan's Political Economy of Defence*. Cambridge, U.K.: Cambridge University Press, 1990.

James, Morrice. *Pakistan Chronicle*. New York: St. Martin's Press, 1993.

Joeck, Neil. *Maintaining Nuclear Stability in South Asia*. New York: International Institute for Strategic Studies, Oxford University Press, 1997.

Kapur, Ashok. *Pakistan in Crisis*. New York: Routledge, 1991.

———. *Pakistan's Nuclear Development*. London: Croom Helm, 1987.

Kusano, Nobuo, comp. *Atomic Bomb Injuries*. Tokyo: Tsukiji Shokan Company, 1995.

Lifton, Robert Jay, and Richard Falk. *Indefensible Weapons: The Political and Psychological Case Against Nuclearism*. New York: Basic Books, 1982.

Mahmud, Farhat. *A History of U.S.-Pakistan Relations*. Lahore, Pakistan: Vanguard, 1991.

Makhijani, Arjun, Howard Hu, and Katherine Yih. *Nuclear Wastelands: A Global Guide to Nuclear Weapons Production and its Health and Environmental Effects*. Cambridge, Mass.: MIT Press, 1995.

Malik, Hafeez, ed. *Dilemmas of National Security and Cooperation in India and Pakistan*. New York: St. Martin's Press, 1993.

Malik, Iftikhar Haider. *State and Civil Society in Pakistan: Politics of Authority, Ideology, and Ethnicity*. New York: St. Martin's Press, 1997.

McGrath, Allen. *The Destruction of Pakistan's Democracy.* New York: Oxford University Press, 1996.

McMahon, Robert J. *The Cold War on the Periphery: The United States, India, and Pakistan.* New York: Columbia University Press, 1994.

Moshaver, Ziba. *Nuclear Weapons Proliferation in the Indian Subcontinent.* New York: St. Martin's Press, 1991.

Mueller, John. *Retreat from Doomsday: The Obsolescence of Major War.* New York: Basic Books, 1989.

Norris, Robert S., Andrew S. Burrows, and Richard Fieldhouse. *Nuclear Weapons Databook vol. 5-British, French, and Chinese Nuclear Weapons.* Boulder, Colo.:Westview Press, 1994.

Pakistan's Security and the Nuclear Option. Islamabad: Institute of Public Policy Studies, 1995.

Quester, George. *Nuclear Pakistan and Nuclear India: Stable Deterrent or Proliferation Challenge?* Carlisle Barracks, Penn.: Strategic Studies Institute, United States Army War College, 1992.

Rahman, Mushtaqur. *Divided Kashmir: Old Problems, New Opportunities for India, Pakistan, and the Kashmiri People.* Boulder, Colo.: Lynne Rienner Publishers, 1996.

Reiss, Mitchell. *Bridled Ambition: Why Countries Constrain Their Nuclear Capabilities.* Washington, D.C.: Woodrow Wilson Center Press, 1995.

Rizvi, Gowher. *South Asia in a Changing International Order.* Newbury Park, Calif.: Sage Publications, 1993.

Rizvi, Hasan-Askari. *Pakistan and the Geostrategic Environment: A Study of Foreign Policy.* New York: St. Martin's Press, 1993.

Schwartz, Stephen I. *The U.S. Nuclear Weapons Cost Study Project.* Washington, D.C.: Brookings Institution, 1997.

Shafqat, Saeed. *Civil-Military Relations in Pakistan: From Zulfiqar Ali Bhutto to Benazir Bhutto.* Boulder, Colo.: Westview Press, 1997.

Smith, Christopher. *The Topography of Conflict: Internal and External Security Issues in South Asia in 1993.* London: Brassey's, 1993.

Spector, Leonard S. *The Spread of Nuclear Weapons 1985: The New Nuclear Nations.* New York: Carnegie Endowment for International Peace, Vintage Books, 1985.

———. *The Spread of Nuclear Weapons 1986–1987: Going Nuclear.* Cambridge, Mass.: Carnegie Endowment for International Peace, Ballinger Publishing Company, 1987.

———. *The Spread of Nuclear Weapons 1987–1988: The Undeclared Bomb.* Cambridge, Mass.: Carnegie Endowment for International Peace, Ballinger Publishing Company, 1988.

Spector, Leonard S., and Jacqueline R. Smith. *Nuclear Ambitions: The Spread of Nuclear Weapons 1989–1990.* Boulder, Colo.: Westview Press, 1990.

Tahir-Kheli, Shirin. *India, Pakistan, and the United States: Breaking With the Past.* New York: Council on Foreign Relations, 1997.

———. *The United States and Pakistan: The Evolution of an Influence Relationship.* New York: Praeger, 1982.

The Military Balance 1996/97. London: The International Institute for Strategic Studies, 1996.

United Nations Development Programme. *Human Development Report 1997.* New York: Oxford University Press, 1997.

Weiner, Myron. *The Politics of Social Transformation in Afghanistan, Iran, and Pakistan.* Syracuse, N.Y.: Syracuse University Press, 1994.

Wirsing, Robert. *India, Pakistan, and the Kashmir Dispute: On Regional Conflict and its Resolution.* New York: St. Martin's Press, 1994.

Wolpert, Stanley. *Zulfi Bhutto of Pakistan: His Life and Times.* New York: Oxford University Press, 1993.

Zaheer, Hasan. *The Separation of East Pakistan: the Rise and Realization of Bengali Muslim Nationalism.* New York: Oxford University Press, 1994.

Articles

Ahmed, Khaled. "Can Pakistan Afford the Bomb?" *Far Eastern Economic Review* 158, 16 March 1995.

Ahmed, Mumtaz. "The Crescent and the Sword: Islam, the Military, and Political Legitimacy in Pakistan, 1977–1985." *Middle East Journal* 50 (Summer 1996).

Albright, David. "India and Pakistan's Nuclear Arms Race: Out of the Closet But Not in the Street." *Arms Control Today* 23, no. 5 (June 1993).

Albright, David, and Mark Hibbs. "The Letters of Abdul Khan." *The Bulletin of the Atomic Scientists* 48 (July/August 1992).

Albright, David et al. "India, Pakistan's Nuclear Weapons: All the Pieces in Place." *The Bulletin of the Atomic Scientists* 45 (June 1989).

Arquilla, John. "Nuclear Weapons in South Asia: More May be Managable." *Comparative Strategy* 16 (January–March 1997).

Auster, Bruce B. "Nuclear Arms." *U.S. News and World Report* 109, 15 October 1990.

Bhimaya, Kotera M. "Nuclear Deterrence in South Asia: Civil Military Relations and Decision-Making." *Asian Survey* 34 (July 1994).

Bhutto, Benazir. "India's Smiling Buddha." *New Perspectives Quarterly* 12 (Summer 1995).

———. "Pakistan's Foreign Policy." In *After the Cold War: Essays on the Emerging World Order,* edited by Keith Philip Lepor. Austin, Tex.: University of Texas Press, 1997.

Bilski, Andrew. "In the Shadow of the Islamic Bomb." *Maclean's* 100, 23 March 1987.

Binkley, Cameron. "Pakistan's Ballistic Missile Development: The Sword of Islam?" In *The International Missile Bazaar: The New Suppliers' Network,* edited by William C. Potter and Harlan W. Jencks. Boulder, Colo.: Westview Press, 1994.

Bray, John. "Pakistan: the Democratic Balance Sheet." *World Today* 46 (June 1990).

Burns, John F. "India and Pakistan Seek Cure for Ills Born of an Old Anger." *New York Times (Late New York Edition),* 29 March 1997.

Carranza, Mario E. "Rethinking Indo-Pakistani Nuclear Relations: Condemned to Nuclear Confrontation?" *Asian Survey* 36 (June 1996).

Chellaney, Brahma. "South Asia's Passage to Nuclear Power." *International Security* 16 (Summer 1991).

Crawford, Mark. "Pakistan Thought to Possess Atomic Bomb." *Science* 235, 6 March 1987.

Crovitz, L. Gordon, and V.G. Kulkarni. "Hawks on Both Sides." *Far Eastern Economic Review* 159, 4 April 1996.

Doerner, William R. "Knocking at the Nuclear Door." *Time*, 30 March 1987.

Doherty, Carroll J. "Bid to Sell Jets to Pakistan May Provoke Fight on Hill." *Congressional Quarterly Weekly Report* 52, 9 April 1994.

Fetter, Steve. "Nuclear Deterrence and the 1990 Indo-Pakistani Crisis." *International Security* 21 (Summer 1996).

"France and the Nuclear Free for All." *The Bulletin of the Atomic Scientists* 46 (July/August 1990).

Ganguly, Sumit. "Explaining the Kashmir Insurgency: Political Mobilization and Institutional Decay." *International Security* 21, no. 2, (Fall 1996).

———. "Indo-Pakistani Nuclear Issues and the Stability/Instability Paradox." *Studies in Conflict and Terrorism* 18 (October/December 1995).

Giles, Gregory F. and James E. Doyle. "Indian and Pakistani Views on Nuclear Deterrence." *Comparative Strategy* 15 (April/June 1996).

Gordon, Sandy. "Capping South Asia's Nuclear Weapons Programs: A Window of Opportunity?" *Asian Survey* 34 (July 1994).

Graham, T.W. "The Economics of Producing Nuclear Weapons in Nth Countries." In *Strategies for Managing Nuclear Proliferation: Economic and Political Issues*, edited by Dagobert L. Brito, Michael D. Intriligator, and Adele E. Wick. Lexington, Mass.: Lexington Books, 1983.

Hagerty, Devin T. "South Asia's Nuclear Balance." *Current History* 95 (April 1996).

———. "Nuclear Deterrence in South Asia: The 1990 Indo-Pakistani Crisis." *International Security* 20 (Winter 1995–96).

Hasan, S. Hidayat. "Command and Control of Nuclear Weapons in Pakistan." *Swords and Ploughshares*. 9, no. 1 (Fall 1994).

Henderson, Simon. "We Can Do it Ourselves." *The Bulletin of the Atomic Scientists* 49 (September 1993).

Hibbs, Mark. "U.S. Believes Khushab Still Cold, No Heavy Water Sold by China." *Nucleonics Week*, 3 July 1997.

Holloway, Nigel, "Pressler Under Pressure: U.S. Senator Fights to Maintain Pakistan Sanctions." *Far Eastern Economic Review* 158, 10 August 1995.

Holloway, Nigel, Jonathan Karp, and Matt Forney. "Goin' Ballistic: American Intelligence Reports that Pakistan has Deployed Chinese M-11 Missiles Could Hurt Sino-U.S. Relations and Raise Security Stakes in the Subcontinent." *Far Eastern Economic Review* 159, 27 June 1996.

Hoodbhoy, Pervez. "Can Tritium Lead Towards India-Pakistan Nuclear Peace?" *Dawn*, 5 November 1995.

———. "Inching Towards India-Pakistan Nuclear Peace Via A Tritium Agreement." *INESAP Information Bulletin*, no. 7 (October 1995).

———. "Not by the Bomb." *Newsline* (November 1991).

——— "Nuclear Myths and Realities." In *Pakistan's Atomic Bomb and the Search for Security,*. edited by Zia Mian. Lahore: Gautam Publishers, 1995.

Husain, Ross Masood. "Threat Perception and Military Planning in Pakistan: The Impact of Technology, Doctrine, and Arms Control." In *Military Capacity and the Risk of War: China, India, Pakistan, and Iran*, edited by Eric Arnett. New York: SIPRI/Oxford University Press, 1997.

Hussain, Mushahid. "A Bomb for Security." *Newsline* (November 1991).
Hussain, Zahid. "Carrot Talk." *Newsline* (April 1994).
———. "The Bomb Controversy." *Newsline* (November 1991).
———. "Uncle Sam's New Bait." *Newsline* (April 1994).
———. "Whodunnit." *Newsline* (April 1994).
"India and South Asia." *Current History* 95 (April 1996).
Jones, Rodney. "Pakistan's Nuclear Options." In *Soviet American Relations with Pakistan, Iran, and Afghanistan,* edited by Hafeez Malik. London: Macmillian, 1987.
———. "Pakistan and the United States: Partners After Afghanistan." *Washington Quarterly* 12 (Summer 1989).
Khalilzad, Zalmay. "Nuclear Proliferation and Stability in Southwest Asia." In *Strategies for Managing Nuclear Proliferation: Economic and Political Issues,* edited by Dagobert L. Brito, Michael D. Intriligator, and Adele E. Wick. Lexington, Mass.: Lexington Books, 1990.
Khan, Dr. Abdul Qadeer. "The Spread of Nuclear Weapons Among Nations: Militarization or Development." In *Nuclear War, Nuclear Proliferation, and Their Consequences,* edited by Sadruddin Aga Khan. Oxford: Claredon Press, 1986.
Khan, Lt. Gen. Mujib ur Rehman. "A False Sense of Security." In *Pakistan's Atomic Bomb and the Search for Security,* edited by Zia Mian. Lahore, Pakistan: Gautam Publishers, 1995.
Kulkarni, V.G. "No War, No Peace." *Far Eastern Economic Review* 150, 11 April 1996.
Leventhal, Paul and Brahma Chellany. "Nuclear Terrorism: Threat, Perception, and Response in South Asia." *Terrorism* 11, no. 6 (1988).
Looney, R.E. "Budgetary Dilemmas in Pakistan: Costs and Benefits of Sustained Defense Expenditures." *Asian Survey,* May 1994.
MacFarquhar, Emily. "Nuclear Scares in South Asia." *U.S. News and World Report* 118, 17 April 1995.
Mahmood, Tehmina. "Nuclear Non-Proliferation Treaty (NPT): Pakistan and India." *Pakistan Horizon* 48, no. 3 (July 1995).
Malik, Iftikhar H. "Kashmir Dispute: A Stalemate or Solution?" *Journal of South Asian and Middle Eastern Studies* 16 (Summer 1993).
McDonald, Marci. "A Cloud of Suspicion: Did BCCI Bankroll an Islamic Bomb?" *Maclean's* 104, 19 August 1991.
McGwire, Michael. "Nuclear Weapons Revisited: Is There a Future for Nuclear Weapons?" *International Affairs* 17, no. 2 (April 1994).
Mian, Zia. "The Poverty of Security." In *Rethinking Security, Rethinking Development,* edited by N. Naqvi. Islamabad: Sustainable Development Policy Institute, 1996.
Murphy, Richard W. "Pakistan and the Nuclear Issue." *Department of State Bulletin* 87 (October 1987).
Naim, S.R. "Aadhi Raat Ke Baad." In *Nuclear Proliferation in South Asia: The Prospects for Arms Control,* edited by Stephen P. Cohen. Boulder, Colo.: Westview Press, 1990.
Naqvi, Ali Sarwar. "Pakistan: Seeking Regional Peace and Progress in a Non-Nuclear South Asia." *Arms Control Today* 23, no. 5 (June 1993).

Navlakha, Gautam, Rita Manchanda, and Tapan Bose. "Political Situation in Kashmir: Duped by Media and Government." *Economic and Political Weekly*, 20 July 1996.

Newberg, Paula R. "Dateline Pakistan: Bhutto's Back." *Foreign Policy* 95 (Summer 1994).

———. "Pakistan at the Edge of Democracy." *World Policy Journal* 6 (Summer 1989).

Nordland, Rod. "A Pakistan Bombshell." *Newsweek* 109, 16 March 1987.

"Nuclear Temptations." *The Bulletin of the Atomic Scientists* 49 (June 1993).

Perkovich, George. "A Nuclear Third Way in South Asia." *Foreign Policy* no. 91 (Summer 1993).

———. "Misperception and Opportunity in South Asia." *Studies in Conflict and Terrorism* 19 (October–December 1996).

Quester, George H. "Nuclear Pakistan and Nuclear India: Stable Deterrent or Proliferation Challenge?" *Military Technology* 17, no. 10 (October 1993).

Raphel, Robin. "U.S. Policy Toward South Asia." *U.S. Department of State Dispatch* 6, 27 March 1995.

Rashid, Ahmed. "Bare All and Be Damned: Ex-Army Chief Reveals Nuclear Secrets." *Far Eastern Economic Review* 157, 5 May 1994.

———. "Nuclear Gambit: Sharif's Bombshell Highlights Attempt to Unseat Bhutto." *Far Eastern Economic Review* 157, 8 September 1994.

Reiss, Mitchell. "South Asia and Nuclear Proliferation: A Future Unlike the Past?" *RUSI Journal* No. 138, 6 December 1993.

———. "Nuclear Rollback Decisions: Future Lessons?" *Arms Control Today* 25 (July–August 1995).

Sarkar, Jayanta and Ahmed Rashid. "Proxy War: Pakistan's ISI Alleged to Target India's Northeast." *Far Eastern Economic Review* 157, 20 October 1994.

Sattar, Abdul. "Reducing Nuclear Dangers in South Asia." *Defence Journal* 21, nos. 1 and 2 (1995).

Schulz, John J. "Riding the Nuclear Tiger: The Search for Security in South Asia." *Arms Control Today* 23, no. 5 (June 1993).

Seth, S.P. "The Indo-Pakistan Nuclear Duel and the United States." *Asian Survey* 28 (July 1988).

Shahi, Agha. "Future of the NPT." *Defence Journal* 21, nos. 1 and 2 (1995).

Smith, Chris. "Nuclear Dangers in South Asia." *CDS Bulletin of Arms Control* no. 16 (November 1994).

Smith, Gerard and Helena Coffan. "A Blind Eye to Nuclear Proliferation." *Foreign Affairs* 68 (Summer 1989).

Smith, Hedrick. "A Bomb Ticks in Pakistan." *The New York Times Magazine*, 6 March 1988.

Solingen, Etel. "The Political Economy of Nuclear Restraint." *International Security* 19 (Fall 1994)

"The Subcontinent's Own Cold War." *The Economist* 329, 25 December 1993–7 (January 1994).

Thompson, Mark. "Well, Maybe a Nuke or Two." *Time* 143, 11 April 1994.

Vanaik, Achin. "Nuclear Insecurity in the Indian Subcontinent: An Uneasy Truce." *Bulletin of Peace Proposals* 20 (December 1989).

Weglarczyk, Bartosz. "Atomic Smuggling, cont'd." *World Press Review* 43 (January 1996).

Weinbaum, Marvin G. "War and Peace in Afghanistan: the Pakistani Role." *Middle East Journal* 45 (Winter 1991).

Wirsing, Robert G. "Pakistan's Security in the 'New World Order': Going From Bad to Worse?" *Asian Affairs* 23 (Summer 1996).

————. "The Kashmir Conflict." *Current History*. 95 (April 1996).

Wolpert, Stanley. "Superpower Politics and South Asia." *Harvard International Review* 9 (July–August 1987).

Zimmerman, Tim. "Nuclear Ambitions." *U.S. News and World Report* 120 (12 February 1996).

Other Sources

Arnett, Eric. "Conventional Arms Transfers and Nuclear Stability in South Asia." Paper presented at the Ninth International Summer Symposium on Science and World Affairs, Cornell University, August 1997.

Fact Sheet on Kashmir. Institute of Regional Studies, Islamabad, 21 August 1997.

Joeck, Neil. *Nuclear Weapons Issues in South Asia*. Center for Security and Technology Studies, Lawrence Livermore National Laboratory, STS-43–93, 2 July 1993.

Kardar, Shahid. "Defense Spending: How Much is Enough?" Unpublished manuscript.

Nuclear Nonproliferation Act of 1978. U.S. Public Law 242. 95th Cong., 1st sess., 10 March 1978.

Ramana, M.V. "Effects of Nuclear Weapons: A Case Study of Bombay." Paper presented at the regional meeting of International Physicians for the Prevention of Nuclear War, New Delhi, February 1997.

Spector, Leonard S. "Restrictions on Aid and Military Sales to Pakistan: 1977–1997." In Leonard S. Spector, *Tracking Nuclear Proliferation*. 1996, unpublished manuscript.

United States Code Chapter 39. 22 U.S.C. 2799aa. *Nuclear Enrichment Transfers.*

United States Department of Energy. Office of Environmental Management. *Linking Legacies: Connecting the Cold War Nuclear Weapons Production Processes to their Environmental Consequences*. (Washington, D.C.,1997).

United States Senate. Committee on Foreign Relations. *Interpreting the Pressler Amendment: Commercial Military Sales to Pakistan: Hearing Before the Committee on Foreign Relations*. United States Senate, 102nd Cong., 2nd sess., 3 July 1992.

United States Senate. Committee on Foreign Relations. Subcommittee on Near Eastern and South Asian Affairs. *Conventional Weapons and Foreign Policy in South Asia: Hearing Before the Subcommittee on Near Eastern and South Asian Affairs*. United States Senate, 104th Cong., 1st sess., 14 September 1995.

Index